GREAT SCOTT!

GREAT SCOTT!

The autobiography of Scotland's most capped player

SCOTT HASTINGS
AND DEREK DOUGLAS

MAINSTREAM
PUBLISHING

EDINBURGH AND LONDON

First published in Great Britain in 1996 by
MAINSTREAM PUBLISHING COMPANY (EDINBURGH) LTD
7 Albany Street
Edinburgh EH1 3UG

ISBN 1 85158 893 0

A catalogue record for this book is available from the British Library

Typeset in Garamond
Printed and bound in Great Britain by Butler and Tanner Ltd, Frome

WITH LOVE TO
JENNY, COREY AND KERRY-ANNE

Contents

1

Sixty-two Not Out

New Zealand 1996

A VOLCANIC eruption, a minor earthquake and a hotel fire on our first night in the country. Scotland's 1996 earth, wind and fire tour to New Zealand had it all. This was my fourth time in the country and we encountered some of the toughest rugby I have come up against even in that hotbed of the sport. We experienced problems of our own making both on and off the field and, of course, I played my 62nd game in Scottish colours which meant that I pulled one cap ahead of brother Gavin in the all-time Scottish standings.

There are a large number of crucially important lessons to be learnt from this tour which I will expand upon later, but, first of all I should, perhaps, concentrate on that new Scottish cap record.

Although the record was worth a lot in some people's eyes my main focus was firstly to get to New Zealand, and secondly to beat the All Blacks. New Zealand had never been the happiest of tour destinations for me. This was, as I've said, my fourth time in the country and twice before, as documented elsewhere, I had flown home injured. I have never believed in jinxes, preferring to stick to the notion that getting hurt was simply the unfortunate result of being in the wrong place at the wrong time. However, with the cap record beckoning, I was forced to the conclusion that I might have to reappraise that eminently sensible interpretation of how the fates operate.

We were into the third week of the tour with just the game against a makeshift South Island Divisional XV in Blenheim to go before the selection was due for the first Test against New Zealand in Dunedin. The phone calls started coming in from the Kiwi media who were keen to talk about the Scottish cap record. However, I wasn't keen even to consider the possibility of a record until I had been selected. I must admit I was a wee bit surprised to be selected for bench duty just four days before a Test match but Gregor Townsend and Ian Jardine both had niggling groin injuries which limited the management's scope somewhat.

Ten minutes into the game Graham Shiel took a leg knock and I started warming up, thinking that I would have to go on and play a full game. The injury eventually put him out of the tour but, to his credit, he stayed on. However, as the game developed it was noticeable that he was limping quite badly and just wasn't right. Graham played on until the 57th minute when the decision was taken by the coaches to bring him off. With my first touch of the ball I almost conceded an interception try when the Kiwi winger was pulled down short of the line by Stuart Lang. I had chased back at three-quarter pace in an effort to recover but I wasn't properly warmed up and, with Scotland well in the lead, there was no way that I was going to risk a pulled muscle by overstretching myself.

Then, just after Stuart had pulled off his try-saving tackle, the same winger burst through again and this time I turned to chase him with a vengeance. I caught him from behind but, in an absolute fluke, I slid over the top of him, catching my left knee on a boot stud as I did so.

I looked down and to my horror saw one of the nastiest cuts that I have ever had on a rugby field. The stud had torn a 6-inch, L-shaped gash on the fleshy part of the leg just above the knee. I knew that it was serious straight away and beckoned to the bench that I was coming off. I couldn't believe it. I had been on the field for eight minutes and it was immediately clear that I had no chance at all of making the Test side for Saturday.

The New Zealand injury jinx had struck again – injured at the World Cup in 1987, injured with the Lions in 1993 and now injured with Scotland in 1996 just four days before what was going to be the biggest game of my life. Maybe there was something in this jinx business after all. I couldn't find words to describe the despair and my total bewilderment over what had happened. The only one which seemed to fit the bill was 'why.' Why me? And why now?

Our physiotherapist Martin Rennison and rubs man Tommy McMullan each took an arm and helped me to the dressing-room where tour doc, Jimmy Graham, took a closer look at the damage.

Considering how bad the cut was – it was so deep the muscle was showing – I was surprised that there wasn't more blood, but I was told that when a gash is as deep as this one was the blood vessels go into immediate trauma whereby they close totally, cutting off the supply.

Jimmy told me that I had no chance of making the Carisbrook Test side. I knew that, of course, but I burst into tears nonetheless. I'm not embarrassed or shy about admitting that. I care very deeply about playing for Scotland and about the standard of my performance. Also, although I had tried to maintain a sense of perspective about it, the possibility of becoming Scotland's most capped player of all time had begun to look very attractive indeed.

The entire tour, which hadn't been going particularly well, had been gearing up to that first Test match. That was why we were there. The Test matches were the absolute focus and everything else had been preparation for that. Now, I was out of the opening encounter with New Zealand with no absolute guarantee that I would be fit in time for the second Test a week later.

While I was lying in the dressing-room feeling sorry for myself I received a surprise visit from an old Kiwi friend, David Inch, who had somehow managed to inveigle himself past the stewards. David had visited Myreside and, with another friend, Graham Pittman, had travelled from Nelson, one hour's drive away to watch the game. I was lying on the treatment couch and when I opened my eyes there was David. He had taken a few beers that afternoon and he declared: 'Hi, Scott. What's up, mate?'

I gestured at the gaping cut on my leg. He looked down and that was the last time I saw him. He looked at the ugly gash, almost threw up and left immediately. He telephoned me the following day to say that he was sorry he had beaten such a hasty retreat but his stomach had been no match for the grisly knee.

With Jimmy Graham back in attendance the question which I needed answered immediately was whether I was going to be fit for the second Test. I hardly dared ask because of what the answer might have been but I steeled myself and said to Jimmy: 'Give me some hope. Will I be ready for Auckland?'

Jimmy had put in ten stitches. He is a recently retired orthopaedic surgeon and a top man. I knew that I was in good hands and that if anybody could put me back together again then it was Jimmy. He thought for a moment and said that so long as infection didn't set in then I would be ready in time. I hope I can be excused in the circumstances for thinking firstly about my own position but, with Graham injured as well, both specialist outside centres in the squad were doubtful and the tour was facing a bit of an injury crisis.

Coach Richie Dixon had said to me before the game that I would only go on in extreme circumstances. When Graham got hurt and those circumstances appeared to have arisen, Richie told me to go on and take it easy. The game was well won and no heroics were being called for. I was, though, apprehensive. I had a kind of premonition that something like this would happen and although I was bitterly disappointed I wasn't entirely surprised. As I've said, the one word that kept galloping through my mind was 'why?'.

That night when we got back to our hotel in Blenheim I telephoned my wife Jenny and told her that I had been injured and that I wouldn't make the Test side for Saturday. I told her, too, that Jimmy Graham had given me his assurance that if the wound stayed clear of infection then I would be back in the reckoning for Auckland and that between now and then getting fit for Eden Park was going to be my absolute focus.

Time was going to be the healer. I took two days off training and by the Friday before the first Test I was back doing some light running. That was way ahead of schedule. The original prognosis was that, even all being well, I wouldn't be able to run until three days before the second Test.

I kept up my aerobic fitness in a gym near our hotel in Dunedin and on the morning after the Carisbrook Test I went off on my own to a local park where I did some quite strenuous running. I surprised myself because, once I had loosened up, I did a full sprint session accompanied by the snow flurries of a Southern Hemisphere winter. I knew then that I was back in the frame for the Test in a week's time.

While I was going through my routine a local resident turned up with his ten-year-old son. We got chatting and the father told me that he wasn't very happy with his son's kicking and so they were practising drop-outs, line kicking and grubber kicks. At the end of my session I stripped off and handed over one of my training jerseys. The look of delight on the youngster's face fairly made my day and I returned to the hotel in better fettle than I had been in the five days since the injury in Blenheim.

I hadn't been given any concrete indication that I would, indeed, be in the side for the second Test but the fact that nobody had really forced themselves into contention for a Test berth by means of an outstanding performance in the games leading up to the Tests meant that the selectors were more than likely going to stick with the bulk of the side which had come through the Five Nations.

You still, though, had to prove to the management that you were worthy of selection and, so far as I was concerned, there was still an outside possibility that the selectors would play Craig Chalmers at fly-half and put Gregor Townsend back into the centre. That was always an option and it was one which served to keep all of the centres on their toes.

The team to play in the Eden Park Test was announced to the squad before we left Rotorua for Auckland. I was in and, to be honest, it was all a bit of an anti-climax. I had been chosen to make my record 62nd appearance for Scotland and nobody really came up to congratulate me. Once it became clear that I was fit it seemed that everybody had more or less taken for granted the fact that I would be back in the side. Even in the midst of my delight, though, I did feel sorry for Ronnie Eriksson. Maybe he had won his cap in the first Test through default but he had played well and had enjoyed a very good tour. Once you get one cap you want more and it must have been difficult for him to be left out for Eden Park.

When the names were read out I just sat there quietly, thinking that 62 Test appearances was not a bad record to have but even now, back home in Edinburgh, I don't look upon it as the end of anything. I've got 62 caps and it's a Scottish record but I still want to play more rugby for Scotland. I think much more significant than the 62 caps is the fact that I have been playing Test rugby since 1986. A decade at the top really is an achievement that I am proud of and, to an extent, the record is just something that happened along the way. I doubt very much whether, in the professional years which lie ahead, a player will be able to play international rugby for a decade and more and, as I say, I am very proud of the fact that I have been able to keep my fitness and, even more importantly, my hunger and my enthusiasm intact during the decade that has passed since 1986.

But there was still the business of playing New Zealand to take care of. I had watched in horror at Carisbrook as we went down to a record defeat, 62–31. First and foremost, it had been a fantastic game of rugby and Scotland had played well in spurts but we had let ourselves down very badly by the poor quality of our defence. Our forwards had played well, but without our first-choice centres, Ian Jardine and Ronnie Eriksson, found the angles of running of the NZ backs a challenge. Sitting there in the Carisbrook stand I couldn't help thinking that it was written in the fates that I wouldn't play there. That was where I had been carted in 1987 and again in 1993 and, this time, I hadn't even made it to the pitch.

I kept my eye very much on the opposition because I hoped that I would be back the following weekend and I was trying to analyse the New Zealand game-plan and pinpoint their weaknesses.

I considered that we had to put the half-backs, Justin Marshall and Andrew Mehrtens, under pressure. If we could have done that then there were opportunities to make the pressure tell, too, on Scott McLeod and Frank Bunce. With that achieved there would be less scope for the NZ back three of Jeff Wilson, Christian Cullen and Jonah Lomu to make quite the mark that they had done in their Test against Western Samoa and in the opening international against us.

As it transpired, Lomu was out injured for the second Test and McLeod – who I felt had tended to overrun Bunce and get himself out of position in the first Test – was dropped in favour of Walter Little for Eden Park, but the basic premise remained the same: get to the half-backs and the pressure would spread down the line.

On the morning of the second Test I was extremely apprehensive. I was just about as nervous as I have ever been before an international. Barry Stewart, the 21-year-old who had come in as a late propping replacement for Peter Wright, was also extremely nervous and I don't think I did his nerves any good when I assured him that it didn't get any better. I was just as nervous on the brink of my 62nd cap as I had been before my first Scotland appearance against France when he was still at primary school!

The build-up to the game had gone well but we faced an awesome task. I had always said that to beat New Zealand we would all have to produce the performance of a lifetime. Richie Dixon had got everything spot on and I don't think I have ever been in a Scotland side which was so well prepared. He had given an inspirational team-talk on the Friday night before the game and every one of us believed – irrespective of how it had gone the week before – that this was another ball-game, and we were in with another very good chance to make Scottish rugby history by securing that elusive first victory over the New Zealanders.

It rained on the morning of the match. And then it rained, and rained and rained. I have never seen conditions like it. By the time we got to the ground, the pitch was in danger of flooding and they had the cricket squeegee machine out soaking up the worst of the surface water. When we ran out on to the pitch I couldn't believe how wet it was. There was a gale-force wind howling down the pitch and there were deep puddles lying everywhere – the conditions weren't ideally how you would have envisaged making a record appearance for your country. But the game wasn't about me or my record. It was about the 15 of us playing with total focus for 80 minutes and every single one of us playing the game of our lives. Nothing less would do.

To my utter disbelief, New Zealand kicked off long and made a dream start. We had talked and talked about not letting the ball hit the deck, but from the kick-off Rob Wainwright and Gary Armstrong got themselves at sixes and sevens and by the time Gary had picked up the soaking wet ball he was bundled into touch just short of our line. Within five minutes we had succumbed to a penalty try from a scrummage and we then faced a real uphill struggle. But to the credit of everyone we really stuck to the task and, in the worst conditions that I have ever played an international, we had a superb, physical first half and trailed by just 17–7 at half-time.

We had given away a penalty in the dying moments of the first half which provided a psychological advantage for New Zealand at the turn, but when we got together in a very wet huddle at half-time we still had this self-belief that we could do it. We had seen nothing from the New Zealanders which made us think that they were going to steamroller us. We were playing with the gale in the second half and Richie told us that we still had the opportunity to turn our dreams into reality. We all agreed.

Unbelievably, Gregor put the kick-off dead, and suddenly, New Zealand had a scrum on the half-way line. That put us under pressure straight away. The first two tries, the last penalty of the first half, and both kick-offs were the key moments of the Test match. We spilt ball, which allowed New Zealand to keep the pressure on. Ian Jardine had gone off, to be replaced by Derek Stark – with Tony Stanger moving to centre – and that caused us a certain amount of

organisational bother but nothing which couldn't be handled. The
final scoreline of 36–12 doesn't, I think, tell the entire story. In my
opinion we were worth more than that but, because of errors, forced
and unforced, we allowed ourselves to be put under pressure by, it
has to be admitted, a very good All Black side which in particular
used its scrummage to devastating effect.

We had come away, I like to believe, with honour intact but there
comes a time if we are serious about maintaining our status in the
world game when we have to discard that gallant losers' tag when we
are playing sides from the Southern Hemisphere. We had spoken so
often before that Test about concentration and not making the errors
which let a side into a game. To then go out and make the kind of
silly errors that we had been talking about – and I include myself in
this criticism – is a bit of a travesty in many respects. We all have
responsibility to increase the intensity of our performance and play
as near as dammit an error-free 80-minute game. That is what the
world's best sides do every time they go out on to the pitch.

I'm very passionate about Scottish rugby. I know that we have the
ability to play successfully against the best in the world but we will
never do that by playing 30 or 40 minutes of great rugby and
something less than that for the rest of the time. There isn't the great
gulf between Northern and Southern Hemisphere rugby that the
purveyors of doom say there is. We have the players. We have the
coaches. We're involved in the right kind of personal preparation.
What we don't have is a domestic system which permits us to play at
the same level of intensity, weekend in and weekend out, that our
rivals in the Southern Hemisphere do. That was one of the major
lessons gained during this fascinating tour to New Zealand which I
want to expand upon now.

Four times in nine years. That's how often I've been to New
Zealand, so I think I am qualified to make some observations on
how we in Scotland should learn from the Southern Hemisphere
experience. We had been there for the World Cup in 1987, had
toured there in 1990 and gone back with the Lions in 1993. New
Zealand was, and remains to my mind, the number one rugby
destination in the world.

It begins and ends in Auckland. The international airport is,
invariably, your first port of call and the final Test is traditionally

played on Auckland's Eden Park. In between are almost four weeks of travelling, two matches and two different towns every week. Touring in New Zealand is of necessity an arduous business. The road and rail infrastructure is not of the best and so internal flights in small aircraft, packing and re-packing twice a week, is the tourists' lot. The baggage, incidentally, travelled in a truck, which invariably meant packing it the night before departure.

Our itinerary had seemingly been designed to enable us to see every blade of grass of a country whose two islands are well over 1000 miles from top to bottom. With hindsight we were, perhaps, naïve to accept the schedule which the New Zealand union had placed before us. Wanganui, in the North Island, was the venue for our opening game. Then we flew to the extreme north-east at Whangarei and back south to Hamilton. Next, we flew to Invercargill at the southernmost tip of South Island and immediately travelled north over the entire length of South Island to Blenheim. From there we did an immediate about-turn to fly back down to Dunedin then north again to Rotorua and, finally, to Auckland. The travelling, which invariably could not be done without at least one change of aircraft on any given leg, undoubted begins to take its toll after a while. That was the schedule which the NZRFU had prepared but it was also the one which the SRU had accepted so we have no grounds for complaint. However, it would surely have made sense to have approached the tour in an ordered geographical manner playing at each venue as it came up on the map rather than being shunted around the country like a pin-ball gone mad. It would be no bad thing if, when next the Kiwis come to Scotland, they could be shown a bit of the country with games in Inverness or Aberdeen, Ayr, Langholm and Dundee, before they make it to Murrayfield. The quality of opposition also had been a bearing on the tour. Scotland always rise to the challenge, and we tend to perform to the quality of the opposition. Outwith the Test matches, only Waikato played an open and expansive game, whereas against Northland and Southland we got dragged down a peg or two.

As the tour went on it became apparent that there just wasn't the kind of interest in us as tourists as there had been during my previous visits. On previous tours whenever we hit town and went out for our first training session the news spread like wildfire and within half an hour a large crowd would have gathered. This time, because the

Super 12 tournament was still on, with Auckland about to play Natal in the final, we were a bit of an afterthought until such time as the Auckland Bulls had seen off the Natal Sharks and until the Western Samoans, whose tour overlapped with ours, had been disposed of by the All Blacks.

Comparisons are invariably odious but New Zealand in 1996 was not a patch on the Scotland tour there in 1990. A good balance was struck on that post-Grand Slam campaign which meant that the whole touring experience was just so much more enjoyable.

What I think has to be said is that, although in comparative terms the opposition we met in 1990 was of a generally higher standard, we had additional factors to contend with in 1996 which were always going to make it a tougher touring experience.

For one thing the itinerary, simply in terms of the travelling, was tougher in 1996. But more importantly, in the most recent tour, we were meeting New Zealand players who had come straight off a three month involvement with the Super 12 series involving provincial sides from New Zealand, South Africa and Australia. This meant that, whereas previously we were catching the New Zealanders 'cold' at the start of their season, they were well up to speed by the time we arrived in 1996.

Additionally, and perhaps even more importantly still, we had new laws to contend with as soon as we arrived in New Zealand whereas the Kiwis had been playing to the new legislation right through the Super 12s. Touring in the Southern Hemisphere has always meant coming to terms with the domestic referees. This time it was no different but, in many ways, the difficulties we experienced in conforming to Southern Hemisphere law interpretation was made even more difficult by the refereeing concept which All Black coach John Hart terms 'added value'.

Referees in New Zealand are now expected to add to the entertainment value of a game. How do they do this? Well, basically, the ref will decide, seemingly on the spur of the moment, whether he is going to stop the game for this infringement or that. It makes for inconsistency and is very, very difficult to come to terms with.

None of the above should be read as excuses for how we performed over there. We knew before we left what we would be up against but until we had actually set foot on New Zealand soil I don't think that even those of us who had been there before really appreciated how much the Southern Hemisphere game has advanced. It has done so to such an extent – on the back of their existing provincial championship and the new Super 12 series in which the country's top players are 'drafted' by the NZRFU to make up the five Kiwi sides in the tournament – that virtually all of us who were on the tour party have returned home more convinced than ever that, if we are to maintain our place in the world's top half-dozen rugby nations, then there will have to be a far-reaching revamp in the Scottish domestic structure.

I said much the same thing when I returned from the Scotland tour to Australia in 1992, but there just has to be some kind of meaningful structure between club and Test rugby. The gap is now, more than ever, just too wide for our players to go straight from playing club games – even via the inter-district championship – to the Test arena. During the 'clubs or districts in Europe' debate which raged in Scotland in the early months of 1996 I was in the clubs' camp. I felt that it should be clubs and not district sides which flew the saltire in the European Cup competition. To an extent, that is still my position, and I await with great interest the outcome of the SRU's decision to place greater emphasis on district rugby, which they announced in the late summer of 1996.

Whether the SRU can ever overcome the parochialism which afflicts the Scottish game to enable such a structure to be put in place is, of course, the 64,000-dollar, question but after our experiences in New Zealand – when the standard of rugby we encountered in the provincial games and, without doubt in the Test matches, was higher than anything we had experienced before – I am convinced that this has to be the way forward for the Scottish game.

When the tour itinerary was announced it was clear that, on the face of it, it could have been tougher in terms of the opposition we were to meet but that notion was quickly dispelled, as I've said, when we confronted the Super 12 and new law factors. The tour opener was against third-division Wanganui – where we had our hotel fire and a minor earth tremor – whom we disposed of 49–13. But it was a ring-rusty performance from Scotland and it was difficult from that one game to gauge just how tough the upcoming matches were going to be.

Against Northland in Whangarei, we faced slightly stronger opposition and fielded, accordingly, what we felt was a stronger

Scottish line-up. For the second game in succession we played under floodlights and in Whangarei the rain fell in torrents throughout. This was my first game on tour and we made far too many errors. Often you find that when someone has made a mistake there is another player there who can clean up the mess to get you back into the game. Against Northland that didn't happen. We just made mistake after mistake. Small things like knock-ons and spilled passes just added up to a very unconvincing performance and one thing led to another, most of them bad. It wasn't until the 79th minute that the first try of the game was scored and that, I think, sums up just what a frustrating experience it had been for us, but less so for Northland who, rightly from their perspective, were happy with their 15–10 win however it was achieved.

That performance simply wasn't good enough. We weren't coming to terms with the refereeing and at training we had to put in place strategies which took account of Southern Hemisphere interpretations. Lifting was being allowed in the lineout and at the tackle situation it was virtually a free-for-all with almost any means being allowed in the effort to retrieve and recycle the ball.

The third game, against Waikato, was always going to be our third 'Test'. Since Southland had been relegated to the second division, Waikato were our only first-division opposition and it was going to be essential that we performed well against the side which had a proud tradition of lifting tourists' scalps, most recently that of the 1993 Lions.

The mid-week timing of the game was problematical in that it posed selection problems for the management. We had already fielded a stronger side against Northland but Waikato also demanded a near Test-strength selection on our part, with Southland to follow just a few days later.

Again I was playing, and we entered the game, having prepared well on the training paddock, against a very professional and equally well-prepared Waikato outfit. The game was played in magnificent conditions and we stormed ahead to a well-earned lead only to suffer the old malaise of letting the opposition off the hook. They got back into the game and we drew away from them again only to lose two tries in quick succession and then see our slender lead obliterated in the final minute with a try from a lineout move which they had already used unsuccessfully in the first half. Waikato were on our line when they took clean 'off the top' ball, carried it round the front, took out Kevin McKenzie with a premeditated professional foul and went over unopposed for the try. We disputed the try because we were certain that number 8 Dion Muir had put a foot in touch. However, the try stood and we had been beaten 39–35.

Strangely, and uniquely, NZ Sky TV, who were broadcasting every game, never showed a replay of the 'try' which merely heightened our suspicions that it hadn't been a try at all. Nevertheless, the fact of the matter is that Waikato should never have been allowed to get within striking distance of us and it was so frustrating to have lost after having played some fantastic rugby. We desperately needed a convincing win at that stage in the tour but, through our own shortcomings, we had denied ourselves the fillip that a win over Waikato would have provided.

Next, we faced the long trek down to Invercargill to play Southland. Again, the rains fell and, despite the common misconception that this is to Scotland's liking, we would much rather have been playing on a firm pitch and with the sun on our backs. We stormed into the lead but still didn't possess the killer instinct required to put the opposition away. Nevertheless, 31–21 in our favour was a pleasing result even if we all realised that we still had a bit to do with the first Test just a week away.

The South Island Divisional XV, which we defeated 63–21 in Blenheim, was of course the scene of my injury which I have documented elsewhere, and then it was back down to Dunedin for the first Test at Carisbrook. I have already given my impressions of that 62–31 defeat which, even allowing for the scoreline, I reckon is one of the most exciting Test matches Scotland have played in recent years. As I've already recounted, we let ourselves down by poor first-up tackling and the scoreline, which suggests an absolute roasting, fails to give us the credit which we were due. It's the scoreline which goes into the record books, though, and there will be no mention there of how well Scotland played.

Our 35–31 victory over Bay of Plenty was preceded by the eruption of Mt Ruapehu which cast a volcanic cloud over our pre-match training session, and then it was back up to Auckland for the second Test and my Scottish record 62nd cap. I hope still to have a season or two left in me at international level but the likelihood is that I will never return to New Zealand on rugby business. It is my favourite touring destination despite the fact that, since 1987, it has caused me so much heartache. In a sense it was fitting that I should capture the record there. The Land of the Long White Cloud certainly owed me a favour and a 62nd cap at Eden Park is just about as good a favour as that rugby-daft country could provide.

This was Scotland's first tour of the professional era and as such there was much less extra-curricular activity than had been the case on previous trips. Generally on tour, once the training is over, it is the custom for the squad to take in some of the local sights – visit a vineyard, go white-water rafting – anything to take the mind off the intense business of rugby for an hour or so.

That didn't happen to any great extent on this tour and, in my opinion, the trip suffered because of that. We travelled under the management of the SRU's director of rugby, Jim Telfer. Now Jim, who is a former Scotland captain, a British Lion and one of the most successful coaches in the history of the Scottish game, is a rugby man through and through. He is also a former headmaster and, rather unfortunately, his headmaster-ish traits tended to show through when we were away.

Jim is a very hands-on kind of person. He was manager but it was difficult to escape the conclusion that he would like to have been coach as well. A similar kind of thing happened with the Lions in 1993 when Geoff Cooke, as manager, liked nothing better than to get into his track suit when Ian McGeechan and Dick Best were the actual coaches. Although on that occasion, Geoff managed the tour well.

I feel that Jim was too keen to manage the players, which should really be the role of the coaches, rather than manage the tour which is the more normal function of the tour manager. Throughout the trip this duality of purpose on Jim's part led to conflicts between the players, the management and the coaches. Jim ran a very tight ship. Everybody got up for breakfast at the appropriate hour, which was generally between seven and eight. That didn't meet with the approval of some players who liked an occasional lie-in, but that is a minor point and there is a lot to be said for an early start because it allows the medics to get their work over and done with before training.

We were also on a very strict diet. To me it makes sense. I always eat a lot of pasta and rice and balance the intake of red and white meat, but, with little or no meat, the meat-eaters on tour weren't greatly enamoured of rugby's *nouvelle cuisine*. There were even a few extremist carnivores who sneaked down early in the morning to have illicit fried bacon for breakfast before the food patrol arrived!

The idea was good in principle, but the implementation dire. During the Five Nations there was a responsible and relaxed attitude to food and drink, but to go from one extreme to another, under the excuse 'that this was the professional way' was just taking things too far. Healthy eating is something which I have been advocating for years and, to a large extent, the high-carbohydrate food which we were taking on board was essential for the twice-daily training routine that we followed for most of the trip. The nature of the diet, though, was a bone of contention for some players.

The demon alcohol – or rather the state of confusion which existed over whether this was meant to be a 'dry' tour or not – was another factor which meant that we conspired to make life difficult for ourselves. We had been advised not to drink alcohol on the 40-hour trek to New Zealand. That makes sense because it helps to nullify the effects of jet-lag. During the first week of the tour, some of the senior players, medics and the like, called a management meeting to discuss the drink issue. Jim – mistakenly – had heard that the All Blacks had steered clear of booze during their successful Hong Kong Sevens campaign and he was of a mind that we should do likewise. He is a very intense and passionate rugby man and he explained that, for some of us, the tour represented our final chance to lodge that historic victory over New Zealand. If a five-week period of alcohol abstention could help in achieving that goal then he reckoned it was a price worth paying.

As players, we maintained that the primary consideration was, surely, to strike a balance which satisfied everyone. It didn't mean the end of the world if we swore off the drink for a month but, sometimes, in the course of a high-pressure rugby tour, a civilised evening with glass in hand is a perfect way to relax, and an ideal way to promote team spirit, As in all things, moderation was the key. In fact, top players now drink very little. During the Five Nations, when I was first involved, it was the norm to have a beer on the Friday night before a game. Nowadays, only two or three of the team touch alcohol prior to a game.

The ironic thing was that, unbelievably, while we were discussing this in Jim's hotel room, we were all on soft drinks while he was getting stuck into a can of Steinlager. The situation was never really resolved but the myth persisted in the NZ media and even in some sections of our own Press, that we were on a 'dry' tour. The consequence was that whenever we left our hotels for a quiet drink in nearby bars even the bar staff were treating us like we were clandestine boozers sneaking out for a few beers on the sly.

After our opening game against Wanganui a few of the boys were a bit on edge as to whether or not they were allowed a beer. Jim told those who had been playing that they could have one, but just the one, mind.

Then, next time out, when we were beaten by Northland in Whangarei in one of the worst games that I have ever played in, we were hauled back to our hotel immediately after the official reception and given a stern dressing-down by the manager. Everything he said was true. We had not played well. We had allowed inferior opposition to beat us 15–10 and we deserved the harsh words which Jim delivered. I agreed with everything he said. However, the headmaster-ish element in his make-up was rearing its head again and he told us that we were all to go off to bed. Immediately.

We were being sent to bed early! I couldn't believe it. Okay, this was the first professional tour in the history of the Scottish game, but being sent to your room was surely taking things too far. I believed that we were behaving as model professionals and it was probably going to be the case that, after such a disappointing defeat, very few of the players would have felt like going out for a post-match drink anyway, but to be told – almost like naughty schoolboys – that you were to go straight to bed was a bit hard to take.

By the time we reached Hamilton for the third game of the tour against Waikato, the whole alcohol thing was becoming absurd. We went out for an Italian meal as a squad and when some of us said that we would like to have a glass of wine with the meal Jim said 'No'. Rob Wainwright, as captain, had a quiet word with the manager and he relented, but just to the extent of a glass or two per player.

And it was in Hamilton that the whole 'booze-ban' fiasco really blew up in our faces. We lost to Waikato 39–35 in what, for me, was the most disappointing game of the tour. Once again we had played well in spells only to allow the opposition to come back into contention when they should have been long since dead and buried.

The Wednesday night after that game had been earmarked in advance by the management as the time when we could have a late night. Team sponsors The Famous Grouse had laid on a few promotions in bars around town and players were to go along to make personal appearances, sign autographs and that kind of thing.

Following our hugely disappointing defeat at the hands of Waikato I certainly didn't feel like making it a late night and I was back at the hotel in good order and at a respectable hour. However, it transpired that, on the basis of getting a 'Scots break booze ban' story, a freelance journalist in Hamilton had been staking out the team. He had followed a lot of the players, noting which bars they had gone to, what they had been drinking, and what time they had got back to the hotel.

The story was sold to Scotland's mass circulation tabloid, the *Daily Record*, and there we were in a situation with the country's international stars being accused of drunken revelry in the immediate aftermath of a dreadful defeat and – more importantly – breaking the tour booze ban. That affair really did affect morale. We now felt that we were under unnecessary scrutiny wherever we went. The perceived no-drink policy had come back to haunt us. As we had tried to point out right at the outset, our stance should have been that it wasn't a 'dry' tour but the players would be drinking in moderation. That was the statement which we had wanted released after that first management meeting right at the start of the tour. It wasn't done and the issue hung over us – if you'll pardon the pun – for the rest of the trip.

Jim's decision, also, to display in the team room on the morning of the Waikato game some clippings from the UK newspapers also caused some consternation among the party. There were two in particular which would have been better kept until after we had played what was the most important provincial game of the tour. The first concerned the training incident when Damian Cronin had been involved in a dust-up with Graham Ellis. Now, I'm not going to condone what Damian did – and especially not the fly kick to the head which he laid on Ellis – but headlines like 'Crazed Cronin beats up his own player' are not entirely conducive to achieving a good team spirit on the morning of a big game.

Similarly, a cutting from the *News of the World* headed something like 'Half-wits – Hastings slams Scotland flops' doesn't do much for team morale either. What had happened in this case was that I had given an interview to one Scottish journalist after our defeat by Northland in which I had said that given the conditions, Gary Armstrong and Craig Chalmers should have kicked a wee bit more. The interview had been passed around other members of the Press party and the *News of the World* story, which quoted me out of context and which put a brutal 'spin' on my comments which wasn't warranted, was the result. That story threatened to sour my relationship with Craig and I had to apologise to him and Gary for the interpretation which the paper had placed on my comments. We could have done without such distractions just hours before what was, at that point, the biggest game of the tour.

I'm a very experienced rugby tourist and I would have to say that this visit to New Zealand was characterised by the lack of what we might call 'good times'. Maybe that's the way the game is going to go in the professional era but, for the younger players especially, the marked lack of any kind of social side to the tour was something which we all missed. On every tour that I've been on previously – with Scotland or the Lions – there has always been a fine balance struck between the rugby and the off-field activities. The fact that, on previous tours, we were able to enjoy ourselves off the pitch was in no way detrimental to the rugby we played. All work and no play makes Jack a very dull boy indeed and, for the purposes of a five-week tour, rugby is work.

Jim Telfer is a man for whom I have respect. His contribution to the cause of Scottish rugby is above and beyond reproach. In fact, so central has Telfer been to the well-being of the Scottish game, that I shudder to think where we would have been if he hadn't been around.

However, man-management is not his strong point and he should not have been managing that tour to New Zealand – or rather, he should not have been managing the players which is the job of the coaches, not the manager. Jim found it hard to believe that the 30 young men under his leadership were not so consumed by the game as he is. But that is, quite simply, because no one in the world is so utterly devoted to the game to the exclusion of almost everything else, as Jim Telfer.

The frustrations within the party came to a head of sorts after the fourth game of the tour against Southland in Invercargill. We had crunched out a not-very-convincing 31–21 victory in the face of some fine tactical play by Southland's All Black international-points-scoring-record holder Simon Culhane.

We were glad to have got the win but, again, we had played well only in spells. We just didn't seem to be able to put together an absolutely convincing 80-minute performance. Anyhow, after the game, Jim told us that he wanted us back at the hotel for a meeting. We trooped into the team room straight from the ground still dressed in our 'number 2s'. Rob Wainwright, Damian Cronin, Craig Chalmers, Doddie Weir and Kevin McKenzie and I voiced our concerns about how the tour was going. We vented our frustrations about the whole trip – how the itinerary was working against us, how the drink issue had served only to lower morale and how Jim's shadow was hanging over the coaches to such an extent that, up until that point, Richie's assistant David Johnston hadn't had the opportunity to make the kind of contribution which a man of his talent really demanded.

We just wanted the opportunity to have some time to ourselves, perhaps to get a few sight-seeing trips organised to let us unwind. Jim questioned our attitude and willingness to raise our game in the days ahead and Kevin and I both declared that this was an unfortunate slur and that the commitment of the players had been absolutely superb. What was now needed, we said, was a day off – a day in which we could have done something that would have released the tensions which were building up within the squad. Jim wanted us to train, play, eat, drink and sleep rugby 24 hours a day. When we weren't doing that he wanted us to watch videos of our own performances, the opposition in action, and our own training sessions.

After the defeat by Northland we had met the following morning to watch a video of the game. There was so much discussion as to what had gone wrong that after 45 minutes we had watched only ten minutes of actual play. It was a very intense meeting and there were a lot of harsh words spoken. Later, Jim said he was disappointed that we had not, as a team, watched the rest of the game on video. When we travelled from Whangarei to Hamilton, unknown to him, we had all decided that we had seen enough and watched a Hollywood blockbuster instead.

I know Jim well enough to tell him where I think the tour went wrong and we have had discussions about it since. To some extent, by winning just one of our first three games (defeating Wanganui but losing to Northland and Waikato), we made it difficult for ourselves. Life would have been a hell of a lot easier if we had beaten Northland and Waikato as we should have done. Victory over first-division Waikato, in particular, would have gone a long way towards enhancing our credibility in the eyes of the New Zealand public and would have given a boost to morale within our own camp.

I wonder whether any of the behind-the-scenes tension really affected the results we achieved on the park. But there are two kinds of tour: the happy tour and the not-so-happy tour. Personally, being older and having seen much of it before, I enjoyed the trip, but if you were to take a survey among the squad as a whole, then I reckon that at least half of them would say that they were disappointed by the experience. And that really is a great, great shame.

2

The Ref was Bi-est!

CHILDHOOD IN EDINBURGH

I WAS once asked in one of those player-profile questionnaires to nominate my worst moment in rugby. 'Finding out that Gavin was my brother,' I replied. Not true. Well, not most of the time anyway.

By the time that I came along on 4 December 1964, Gavin was almost three and there was an older brother still, Graeme, who was nearly five. Gavin's appearance must have taken the wind out of Graeme's sails and when I made my appearance both of them must have wondered what on earth was going to happen next. And what did happen next was that Ewan appeared a couple of years later. Four sports-daft boys, all as competitive as sin, eight years from first to last.

Our mum, Isobel, and dad, Clifford, deserve a medal apiece for having successfully set their four wilful boys off in the right direction. We lived in a big sandstone villa in the Merchiston district of Edinburgh. We had a very comfortable, middle-class childhood where hard work was a virtue, good manners were considered to be essential and where school, the scouts, the church and sport were the mainstays of our weekly routine.

But most of all sport. Our house in Merchiston Place had a reasonably-sized back garden. It is probably not nearly as big as I thought it was when I was a youngster but, depending on the season and whatever sport was showing on television at the time, it was our Murrayfield, Wembley, Wimbledon and Lord's. The cricket 'season' was particularly fraught. Broken windows were often the order of the day and the culprit would have his pocket money stopped to pay for the repair. Then, if the ball went into the next-door garden, there would inevitably be a battle over whether the batsman who struck it over the wall should go and retrieve it, with six runs and out, or whether the bowler who had sent down such an appalling delivery should be the one to go and ask whether we could have our ball back again, please.

For wet days we had a sports room at the back of the house where darts and table tennis were on offer. Inevitably, fisticuffs would break out when it came to who had scored the winning point in table tennis. The loser would immediately demand 'the best of three' and then it would be 'best of five'. To say that none of us liked to be beaten would be the understatement of the century. Get the picture? There was never a dull moment in the Hastings household.

It would, then, be fair to say that life was hectic. Even when we went on holiday there would be no let-up in the madly competitive environment that we all so much enjoyed. We went on summer holidays as a family to Strontian, Nethy Bridge, or Grantown-on-Spey. At Grantown our folks used to rent a house and right across the road was a sports-mad youngster's dream. The football pitch was next to the tennis courts, which was next door to the bowling green, and beyond the tennis court was the golf course.

Years later Graeme was the first to achieve recognition outside the biased confines of our own front room when, in 1978, he was capped for Scottish Schoolboys. Gavin and I both followed suit and we have all played for Watsonians, including Ewan, although he never took his rugby as seriously as his big brothers.

Graeme now lives in Australia, where he has played for the Melbourne Rugby Club and Victoria State side, so we don't see as much of him as we would like to. The rest of us now get on better than we have ever done in our lives. As you grow older brotherly hate tends to turn, via brotherly indifference, to something approaching brotherly love and it would be true to say that we are now all the very best of friends.

I suppose that, to the sporting public, I have always been Gavin's wee brother but, in all honesty, that perception is not something which has ever bothered me. It's true that for most of our sporting lives Gavin has hogged the headlines. Hell, he's even doing it now that he has retired and is playing American football for the Scottish Claymores. But I have been immensely proud of what we have all achieved. The Hastings boys have become synonymous with success in Scottish rugby and I am just as proud of Gavin's achievements as he is of mine.

I would be lying, though, if I denied that there wasn't – at least in our early years – a keen sense of rivalry between Gavin and me. It really couldn't be any other way. Graeme was the oldest with Ewan the youngest and Gavin and I sandwiched in between. Birthdays stick out in my memory. Each of us would have a party at home and our pals would be invited along. I recall that I seemed to spend most of the time at my parties battling with Gavin. When I was a youngster I had a really hot temper and Gavin would tease me until I flipped. Then there would be no stopping me until blood had been spilt. Sadly, because Gavin was almost three years older, it was almost always mine.

I daresay that we weren't any better or worse than any other household containing four boisterous young boys and all of that is now very firmly in the past. Indeed, since Gavin retired from international rugby I have felt an even greater sense of responsibility to keep the Hastings flag flying and to uphold family honour, whether it be in a Scotland or, to a lesser extent, a Watsonians' jersey.

In the spring of 1996 I led Watsonians to rare triumphs on successive weekends at the Gala and Melrose Sevens, but the perception from quite a number of people was that I had done something which Gavin had never done. It's not something which grates with me and, maybe, it is an inevitable result of having a famous big brother, but I can honestly say that having the shadow of Gavin looming over me has never been an issue.

Nevertheless, looking back, it must often have seemed to passers-by in Merchiston Place that World War III had broken out. If it wasn't Graeme picking on Gavin then it was Gavin picking on me. I, then, had no alternative but to pick on poor Ewan. Psychologists might call it sibling rivalry. Our long-suffering mum called it something else entirely! There was a great deal of rivalry and, really, it was all about winning. We all wanted to be best.

There were, though, quieter and more contemplative moments. Sunday walks were a big thing in the Hastings household. Despite all appearances to the contrary in view of what I've just said about our internecine warfare, we had quite a strict upbringing in many respects. Both parents insisted that we went to Sunday school, church or Bible class. I wouldn't say that I'm particularly religious, but, from this distance in time, I can see that church attendance did bring some order to our lives and, even now, I do experience a sense of warmth and well-being on the altogether-too-infrequent occasions that I present myself at church.

So, after church it would inevitably be off to see Granny Bell and Auntie Bunny for lunch and then, in the afternoon, we would strike out for the Braid Hills or Braidburn Valley for Sunday walks. We would each take a football so it was never, as somebody said about golf, a good walk wasted.

There was strict discipline in the house but with four high-spirited boys to take care of it couldn't be any other way. So much so that by the time I was six or seven there was a duty rota drawn up by my father which assigned many of the household chores to his young brood. Setting the table, walking the dog, making the dog its supper . . . these were our daily tasks.

Inevitably, my earliest specific memories are all about rugby. Myreside, the Watsonians' ground, seemed to be almost the hub of our existence. Dad had played number 8 and lock for the club before he had to retire early with a dodgy back. He and mum were keen golfers and one of my earliest memories is of the entire clan motoring down to Gullane, that East Lothian golfing haven, and site of the Muirfield championship course, 15 miles east of Edinburgh.

There would be six of us, with the dog as a non-playing spectator, hammering balls up and down the links. Sometimes our enthusiasm more than exceeded our expertise and dad taught us one lesson above all others. If your ball went into the rough then you never took your eyes off it. With six of us playing he certainly couldn't afford to fork out for a constant supply of new balls. In fact, I don't recall him ever buying us new balls at all. We were more or less expected to get out into the rough and look for balls that other golfers had given up as lost. I must have been well into my late teens before I realised that golf balls came in cellophane wrappers and looked pristine white with the name of the maker printed clearly on the side.

But golf was just a pastime. Rugby was altogether more serious. We lived nearby Myreside and Saturdays always meant spending the afternoon watching Watsonians. I say 'watching' in the loosest possible sense of the word. We would get our track suits on and meet up with our school pals. In those days, and it is still the case today, there was a great family atmosphere at Myreside. While the FPs were going through their paces we would have our own games going on at the nearby hockey pitches.

My first real contact with the FPs took place not at Myreside at all. Often I would travel across the city to Trinity to visit a pal, Ross MacDonald. We went down to the local playing fields to kick a ball about and stumbled across Watsonians who were playing Trinity Academicals. I must only have been nine or ten, but to this day I can recall going into the changing-hut with Ross and there were these giants in the maroon and white striped jerseys. As boys do, we patted them on the back as they left to do battle with the Accies. We thought they were all heroes.

Similarly, at Myreside when it got too dark for us to continue our games on the hockey pitches, we would retire to the clubrooms for our Cokes and Quavers and settle down to watch the football results on telly. The players would appear for their tea before adjourning to the bar upstairs. Again, as youngsters, we thought they were all giants and we all thought that, one day, that would be us.

There was never much doubt that we would be anything other than Watsonians. My father and his father before him had gone to George Watson's College and that was where we ended up as well. My father, as a canny Scottish chartered accountant, had probably worked out that with school fees to find for Graeme and Gavin he would be as well adding to the family with me and Ewan because that way he would almost certainly qualify for a discount!

Until 1989 the Watsonian Football Club operated as a genuine former pupils concern. Founded in 1875, the club is one of the oldest in Scotland and, for that matter, the world. The club has had 52 players capped for Scotland. We won the Scottish championship for the first time in 1892 and although we are once again riding on the crest of a wave our most successful years were those just before the Great War. Nevertheless, Watsonians have won the Scottish championship on no fewer than 15 occasions and only Hawick and Edinburgh Academicals have a better record.

Rugby, then, ran in the blood and for me it started in 1974 as a nine-year-old with the JB1s at George Watson's College. That was the primary six first team. I was fly-half and captain. Probably here the Hastings name worked in my favour. Graeme and Gavin had both been trailblazers for me at Watson's and they had both proved that they could play a bit. The masters probably thought, here's another Hastings boy, we'll make him captain. Because of all the bounce games that I had already played on those Saturday afternoons at Myreside I wasn't a total novice but my first real, official game of rugby was for the JB1s against old Edinburgh rivals Daniel Stewart's and Melville College, away at Ferryfield.

I can remember the game with absolute clarity because I kept a documentary record of every game that we played. I noted the details in a small notebook – I have it in front of me now – *The Handy Scribbling Tablet, ruled and perforated, British Made.* It tells me that we won 7–0 with a try and a penalty goal on a soaking wet day.

To this day I recall going back home afterwards, still covered in glaur from head to toe, and soaking in a steaming hot bath. For some reason or other we never used the showers after a game but just put our school uniforms back on with the mud from the playing field still clinging to us and worn like a badge of honour. We took it really seriously.

There was great tradition and rivalry associated with those games against other Edinburgh schools and, in fact, the rivals that you would come up against as a nine-year-old – people like Jeremy Richardson, for instance, who played for Edinburgh Academy – you would still be playing against over 20 years later, Jeremy for Edinburgh Accies and me for Watsonians.

However, my *Handy Scribbling Tablet* tells me that our next game was against George Heriot's School, played on the Tipperlin pitch at Myreside. It was the only game we lost all season. There was, though, for that game a sting in the tail. The referee was a Welshman by the name of Bert Shires who was an engineer at Watson's. Heriot's scored in the dying seconds to equalise 12–12.

A guy called John Liddle, who I still bump into from time to time, never allows me to forget what happened next. He stepped forward to take the conversion which would have won the game for them. He missed. To my consternation Bert Shires blew the whistle and said that John should take the conversion again because I had been leaning against the goal-posts. I couldn't believe it. This time John made no mistake. The ball flew straight and true and we lost 14–12.

Our record for the season was played eight, won five, lost one with two games drawn. That wasn't a bad record for our first season but I also note that we played Daniel Stewart's five times which indicates that we were operating to a pretty limited fixture list. That incident with Bert Shires and me leaning against the post cost us an unbeaten season. I've never leaned against a post since!

We were very lucky at school in that we were coached by people who knew what they were talking about and we had the core skills of the game drummed into us from a very early age. Over the years I've built up a bit of a reputation as a solid tackler. Well, that was all based on the work done by people like Bert, Ian Gray and Donald McCuigan, who took the JB1s all those years ago.

For tackle practice we would pair up and one guy would kneel on the ground and the other boy would run at him. You would then make the hit with the shoulder and stick your head behind your partner's backside. It would then just be a simple case of pushing him over, with your head well out of harm's way. I see lots of youngsters when I go down to mini and midi coaching sessions who are a bit intimidated by the physical aspects of the game. But when you put them through that exercise, showing them the safe and, hopefully, painless way to tackle, their confidence grows in leaps and bounds.

It's strange the memories that come flooding back when you embark upon an exercise like this book. In the context of tackling, I've been told time and again that the best and most important tackle I ever made was when I collared Rory Underwood in the 1990 Grand Slam game at Murrayfield. But I know that the best tackle I ever made occurred 15 years before that on a Wednesday afternoon when George Watson's JA1s were playing Morrison's Academy at Crieff. Their winger escaped on a touchline break and I hared off after him. I was pulling him in and as I got to within a couple of yards I suddenly had this mental picture of Gerald Davies pulling off a fantastic diving tackle in, I suppose, a Welsh game against Scotland. I launched myself and got him right around the bootlaces. Copybook stuff. He crashed to earth like a felled pine tree and a certain try was saved. I've made hundreds of tackles in my career against All Blacks and Wallabies and all the rest but, I swear, the best of them all, seen by three men and a dog, was against that unnamed Morrison's Academy winger on a sunny Wednesday afternoon in October 1974.

I was very lucky indeed that I received my schooling at Watson's. It was, and is, a very fine rugby school and, in a sense, because we got first-rate rugby tuition from primary six onwards, we had a head

start on other schools which didn't begin to take the game seriously
until secondary level.

After my first season I couldn't wait for the next to begin. By the
time primary seven came around we had been elevated to the JA1s
and once again I was captain and keeping my match-by-match
records.

At the end of that year, and once again following in the footsteps
of Graeme and Gavin, I was awarded the McIlroy Prize for rugby.
But all the time I was working on increasing my skill levels. Of
course, that wasn't how I looked at it at the time but constant
practice does make perfect and, just because I enjoyed it, I was
almost constantly involved in one form of practice or another. At the
rear of the house we would kick the length of the garden and when
we had managed it with the left foot dad would ask us whether we
could do it with the right foot as well.

Then, with Colin Hunter, a boyhood friend and my JA1s scrum-
half who much later became best man at my wedding and who went
on to play flanker with Watsonians, I would play a game called
gaining ground. To make it more interesting we would force
ourselves to kick off the weaker foot which in my case is the left. So
even at the age of ten I was getting into the habit of using either foot
to kick. The game was just about as simple as you can get. It was
played on the rugby pitch, one on one. The ball was kicked off and
if it was caught on the full then you could take ten paces forward.
You then booted it back upfield and if it went into touch then you
drop-kicked it back into play. You scored by kicking the ball between
the uprights. Once you were within distance you could nominate
whether you wanted to go for goal with a punt, drop-kick or place
kick. You would get one point for a punt, two for a drop and three
for a successful place kick. During the Christmas holidays Colin and
I would play endless hours of gaining ground.

There was a danger amid all of this addiction to sport that my
educational welfare at Watson's might have been neglected. However,
the teachers saw to it that I kept my nose to the educational
grindstone and a recurring theme of my class reports from that time,
and later, was to the effect that Scott was easily distracted and that
he should keep plugging away. Keep trying was the message that
always came through. I'll admit that I was never the brainiest kid
around but I always tried and I like to think that my facility for

dogged perseverance is one that has seen me through quite a number of the challenges that life has thrown at me.

When I graduated to the senior school in 1976 I was still captain of the first team – this time the D1s – and I was still keeping my weekly logs of our rugby fortunes. The season opened on 25 September with a home game against Stewart's Melville – yes, them again – and we won 28–8 or, as my contemporary record puts it: 'A win for us 28–8 and I got a try'.

The following week, against Edinburgh Academy, it was '11–9 to them'. I've also written 'Tries I got – zero, kicks I got, one drop'. We were still playing the same old suspects that we had been meeting every Saturday since primary six. Jeremy Richardson was still putting himself about as one of the giants in the Edinburgh Academy side which went something like five seasons without a defeat, and, truth to tell, we have all grown old together.

I note that the result of our game against Heriot's ended in an 8–4 victory to them but I highlight the fact that we were playing in maroon jerseys instead of our traditional maroon and white hoops that day. On 20 November we were beaten, yet again, by Edinburgh Academy. Our record up until that point was played five, won two, lost three, points for 53, against 67. I had scored 19 points. I also point out, to whom I know not because the records were purely for my personal consumption, that a game – opposition not mentioned – which Watson's had won 50 points to nil was conducted without me!

On 26 February we beat Merchiston Castle School 1–0. How so? I noted: 'This lasted about four minutes because Merchie had to go. We beat them at football for it was a hard pitch'!

On 5 March I excel myself. I write that we lost 14–12 against Heriot's but, in explanation, note that we had suffered at the hands of a 'very bi-est ref' who had disallowed two tries by us and not allowed any 'advantages' or penalties. The tally for that season reads played seven, won three, lost four, although I scrawl underneath that we should really have won four had it not been for the Heriot's ref. My total points for the season were 23 with five tries and a drop goal.

Team-mates at this time included Clive Millar who played for Watsonians and then went on to Kelso where he won a bagful of sevens medals, Remo Maciocia who went on to play for Scottish Schools and Watsonians before a bad neck injury cut short his career, and Ian Torrance who is now in the RAF and who was hooker with Scottish Schools.

My representative career took off when, as a 14-year-old, I was chosen to represent Edinburgh Schools Under-15s against Midlands Schools Under-15s at Pitreavie, although the previous year I had got a trial for the Under-15 side but had played particularly poorly and was desperately disappointed not to be selected. By this time Graeme was already playing for Scottish Schools and Gavin had represented Edinburgh Schools and so, as has been the case throughout my career, I had very definite goals to aim for if I was to emulate my two bigger brothers. In fact, around this time, Graeme was playing for Edinburgh Under-21s, Gavin was captaining the Edinburgh Schools side and I was captaining the Edinburgh Schools Under-15 side. That was according to a newspaper report of the time which added: ' . . . and there is a fourth brother.'

We defeated Midlands Schools 16–7 and, apparently, I converted a couple of tries. Funny that, I had almost forgotten that I used to kick goals. Thanks to Edinburgh's *Sporting Pink* paper for reminding me. The *Pink* was a bit of a Saturday night institution and by the time that we had all cut out the reports of our respective matches it looked like it had been savaged by an origami master on speed. It was always better to get there first. If you didn't then there was a pretty good chance that your match report had been left in tatters with a cut-out from the reverse page. We certainly got our money's-worth from the good old *Pink*.

With each year that passed I was still progressing on the rugby front and it was still my firmly held conviction that, one day, I would play for Scotland. One incident from then in particular stands out. Saturday mornings in our house were a bit like an army getting ready to go on manoeuvres. With four rugby-playing boys, our parents had to shuttle us off in the car to various grounds at varying kick-off times. Once, when I had been picked up from my game and we were returning home, I announced that I would, indeed, play for Scotland. The entire family, Graeme and Gavin to the fore, told me not to be so daft and that there was absolutely no chance of me getting my hands on a Scottish cap. They mocked me mercilessly and I was seething. Silently, I vowed that I would prove them all wrong. The rest, as they say, is history and it is certainly not for me to point out that although he is three years my senior Gavin made his Scotland debut on exactly the same day as me!

By 1980 I had moved from fly-half to full-back and was getting representative honours with the full Edinburgh Schools' side. Despite the fact that I became known as a centre at international level – that is with the exception of one particularly notable occasion when I was drafted on to the wing for Scotland against the All Blacks, of which much more later – I actually played most of my schoolboy rugby at either stand-off or full-back. In fact I was well into my senior career before I made the switch to centre. I played for, and captained, Scottish Schoolboys at full-back and made my senior Watsonians' debut on the wing.

My first taste of the delights of touring came as a 15-year-old with the George Watson's first XV which went to Vancouver Island, Canada, in October 1980. We played four games over there and it was a marvellous experience. I was still keeping detailed records of my expanding rugby career and the front cover of my Canada tour log declares: 'Do not read. Strictly private.' Rather disappointingly, though, the only misdemeanours it has to report are one or two adolescent drinking sessions.

The opposition was St George's School, Shawnigan Lake, McGhee High School and Brentwood College. I was really chuffed as a 15-year-old to get an opportunity to get away on a fully-fledged rugby tour. In those days a tour usually meant spending a weekend away somewhere but there we were on the other side of the Atlantic Ocean. It opened my eyes still further to the worldwide possibilities that rugby had to offer.

The following season I qualified for a trial with Scottish Schoolboys but due to a leg injury I had to pull out. That meant missing the games against Wales and France and it wasn't until the second half of the season that I was pulled in to represent Scottish Schools against Australian Schools at Murrayfield. The Aussies had a fantastic side which included a number of youngsters who went on to become household names in the world of rugby. Michael Lynagh was there, Cameron Lillicrap and Steve Tuynman – who just six months later went on to represent the full international side. These Australians really were something special. We were hammered 34–0 and we all had our eyes opened to the kind of totally athletic rugby that they were then playing in Australia.

I was still plying my trade at full-back and later that season was made captain for the Schools' game against Ireland. Unfortunately, it was a record defeat, 44–0. The game was played at Cork and the Irish captain was one Brendan Mullin. We didn't know it at the time, of course, but that was the start of a long and friendly relationship which encompassed Five Nations' encounters as rivals and a Lions tour as brothers-in-arms in Australia.

The experience of being on the wrong end of a 44–0 drubbing wasn't something that I was used to but, for me, the experience was even more galling because my mum and dad had motored all the way across to Cork to watch me play. They were, I think, the only Scottish parents who had made the huge effort to get across to the Emerald Isle and that was just typical of the manner in which they supported all of us in our rugby careers. They have been our greatest supporters and our most stern critics. They were never pushy – not at all the parents from hell that some rugby sons are saddled with. They allowed us all to develop in our own way but their quiet, unobtrusive support over the years has meant a very great deal to me and I'd like to thank them for all that they did for all of us.

I played four times in all for the Schoolboys side: these two matches against Australia and Ireland, plus outings against Scotland Youth and English Schools. We never had a win but played some good rugby along the way. Adam Buchanan-Smith, who got a couple of caps with Heriot's FP, and, of course, Jerry Richardson, were two of my contemporaries in that Scottish Schools side. Traditionally, the Schoolboys international side has suffered a disappointing wastage rate. Many players who show great promise when they are at school just seem to disappear off the face of the earth. Many of them are lost to the game for ever. They leave school, go off to college or university, or gain employment. The focus of their lives change and they no longer give rugby the priority that they once did, and which they would have to continue to give, if they were to keep climbing the ladder. There's still tremendous scope really to develop schoolboy rugby in Scotland. Ireland have an extremely well-developed schoolboy system and they never fail to produce extremely fine schools' sides.

There's a purity, a rawness and even a beauty, about top-grade schoolboy rugby which gets lost in the senior game. A 'miss one' move still works. It's rather like watching *101 Great Tries from the '70s*. When I watch some of the defensive lapses which allowed some of the great characters like Gerald Davies and JPR to score their superb tries I wince. They were unbelievable tries which profited from disastrous defending and there is just no way that they would be scored nowadays. Defence is now almost a science and it is well nigh impossible to score from first-phase possession. Even to score off second, third or fourth-phase ball can prove difficult, such is the strength of some defences these days. But most schoolboy rugby is played as I imagine the game was played away back in the old days. Players play what's in front of them and the genuinely talented ball-player stands out a mile. That's the real beauty of schoolboy rugby.

I would make a very strong case, too, for schoolboy international matches always to be played as curtain-raisers for senior Tests. That means playing all Scottish Schools games at Murrayfield and, in that way, the boys involved would enjoy an even greater sense of occasion. Far too often schoolboy Test matches are played in the back of beyond and in competition with other domestic games which means that the most they can hope for in the way of crowds are the players' parents, relatives and a few friends.

I know that from as far back as I can remember I have always performed best when there was a big crowd. In a sense it's like showing off. You're saying, look at me, look at what I can do. Sometimes, of course, it doesn't come off and you end up looking like a prize melon, but it's an absolute fact that players who have the inclination and the ability to go all the way find that the bigger the crowd the bigger the boost their personal performance gets. So, come on Scottish Schools Rugby Union, let's really go for it and make schoolboy Test rugby a real showcase for the game. In future make the schoolboy international the curtain-raiser for all Murrayfield games.

3

Howay The Lads

SCHOOLDAYS CAME to an end in the summer of 1982 when I traded the leafy suburbs of Edinburgh for the pleasures of Tyneside, but my journey to Geordie-land, where I was to enrol for a business studies course at Newcastle Polytechnic, went via the delights of Devon and Cornwall.

Watsonians had organised a pre-season tour in tandem with the Under-21 side and, as an only recently ex-schoolboy, I went with them. I made my senior debut with Watsonians on the wing against Devonport Services. Gavin was at full-back and Euan Kennedy, who went on to win full international honours with Scotland, was in the centre. I was also playing alongside blokes like Kenny Ross, Peter Hewitt, Mark Watters, Donald McKill and Ian Nicholson, whom I had watched as a youngster at Myreside. We won 35–18 and I scored a try, so my senior career had got off to a satisfying start. The *Scotsman* newspaper dutifully recorded that I had made a 'promising' debut. It's down there in black and white so it must be true!

I found senior rugby a massive step up from the schools games – and even schools internationals – which had been my staple diet up until then. The physicality of the senior game, especially up front, was a real eye-opener. All of us kids were 'gofers' for the senior players but the up-side of that was that we never had to buy a beer. In fact I had won £150 in one of our fund-raising raffles and so my first experience of senior touring never cost me a penny. I was a pro years ahead of the rest!

Significantly and coincidentally, in view of the move that I was

about to embark upon, I made my Myreside debut, at full-back, for
Watsonians against Tynedale. But I had already decided that, even
although it was just two hours by road from Newcastle to
Edinburgh, it would be better all round if I concentrated on
establishing myself in my new life at the Polytechnic without the
distraction of having to travel home a couple of times each week.

So, for the next couple of years I played most of my rugby in
England. The two clubs in which I was interested were Newcastle
Northern and Newcastle Gosforth. During Freshers' Week at college
I was strolling around wearing a rugby jersey and was directed
towards the College rugby club. Steve Gustard, an ex-Gosforth and
England A winger, was coach of the Poly team. He invited me over
to Gosforth to watch a game. He said that I could have a look
around, have a few beers and meet the President after which I could
make up my mind about joining them.

However, I was keen to get started right away and, with an Irish
friend, David Parkes, I went down to Northern with my kit-bag and
just asked if I could have a game. They put Dave and me into the
fifth XV and the first time I touched the ball I was under the posts
for a try. As I was running back to the half-way line my team-mates,
none of whom was known to me, asked who I played for. I said that
I'd played two or three games for Watsonians. What else, they asked.
I told them that I had captained Scottish Schoolboys. Immediately
one of the guys on the touchline ran over to the first XV pitch and
told the selectors that a Scottish Schoolboy cap had turned up on
their doorstep. We had a good few beers and they sent me away with
membership cards and phone numbers and the very next week I
made my debut with the Northern first XV. Dave only got into the
second XV!

They were playing to a pretty high standard at this time. They had
fixtures against Orrell, London Irish, Boroughmuir, West
Hartlepool, Melrose and so on. The thing that made an immediate
impression on me – and it remains true to this day – was the size of
the forwards in the English game. We had George Longstaff and
Andy James – two huge men, both over 6ft 6in – in the second row
and they were by no means extraordinary on the English club scene.
The sheer physical power of the English forwards was something
that I had never come across before. In truth, I would have to say
that the rugby we were playing at Northern during this period was,

from a backs' perspective, pretty boring stuff. The entire English game was going through a phase of juggernaut packs linked to kicking fly-halves – 'What's that,' I hear you say, 'some things never change' – and for somebody who had been reared on the Watsonian tradition of fluent, running rugby, I found the transition quite hard to make.

I made my first XV debut for Northern against Hartlepool Rovers at full-back on 9 October 1982. Sandy McRae, who went on to play for Edinburgh Academicals, was playing for Northumberland in a county game that Saturday and his absence let me into the side. Right away I got my knuckles rapped by the coach for running the ball out of our territory. 'Don't do that. Just kick it to touch and we'll win the lineout,' he scolded.

Obviously, his admonition didn't have the desired effect because in the very next game, against a Durham University side which included Chris Oti, I threw the ball to myself from half-way, beat a couple of men and then dropped a goal. That kind of opportunism didn't go down well with the coach and, sadly, that is still the case with many coaches who far too often adopt a safety-first attitude. But I'm a great believer in trying the unexpected. If you run the ball 60 metres from deep and, say, a pass is intercepted and the opposition kick 30 metres to touch then you've still made a net gain and, more importantly, you keep the enemy guessing all the time. If you are too stereotyped in your approach then you are going to get absolutely nowhere.

There is no doubt whatsoever that in opting for Northern as opposed to Gosforth I made absolutely the right choice so far as off-field activities were concerned. The social scene at Northern made Gosforth look like a band of monks. Gosforth always grabbed the headlines but we had more fun. The two clubs were situated on either side of the A1 and there was a steady stream of transfers from one club to the other. You would have a player turning out for Gosforth one weekend and then he would enlist with Northern the next, and vice versa. Then he would fall out with Northern and he'd be back with Gosforth a fortnight later.

Within two months of throwing in my lot with Northern I received a call from the Northumberland county side asking if I was available for selection. I was still just 17 and thought this was fantastic. I played for their Under-21 side and, in mid-term, came back to play for Watsonians. Then Watsonians found themselves in serious relegation trouble and at the end of the1982–83 season I went back to Myreside to help keep the club in the first division. By the end of the season I had played over 50 games of senior rugby and appeared 14 times on the seven-a-side circuit. I had played too much rugby and by the season's end I was feeling the strain. That was a sound lesson learnt early in life. When you're 17 you feel indestructible. I was fitter than I had ever been and just never said no whenever I was asked to play.

Today I see young players just like me who never say no and never take a break. You have players turning out for their clubs, age-group district sides, full district sides and age-group internationals. They are playing too much rugby and they will burn themselves out. Often the player isn't the best person to turn down opportunities to play representative rugby. In fact he's the last person in the world to do so. The feeling always persists that if you say no then you won't be asked again. Here, selectors and those in charge of representative sides have to adopt a much more reasonable attitude and realise that young, gifted players will be turned off if too much is asked of them too early.

I was thoroughly enjoying my spell in Newcastle. The Geordies are great folk and I made friends there who are friends for life. Even now, before an international match, a fax will arrive from ex-Northern team-mates wishing me well and it is great that rugby provides this kind of enduring comradeship.

During the summer of 1983 I got my appetite for the game back and, before the start of the season, I was so fit it was almost frightening. I was in great nick when Watsonians went down to Selkirk for the autumn sevens. Then I received another lesson in the ups and downs of a rugby career. We got through to the final against a superb Kelso seven based around Euan Common, Andrew Ker, Bob Hogarth, Eric Paxton and Gary Callander. Andrew Ker, of course, one of the greatest exponents of the abbreviated game that ever lived, is a PE teacher at George Watson's College and is the assistant coach at Myreside. He has now been promoted to coach of the Scotland seven-a-side. squad, and I'm sure he will get more out of his players than his predecessors.

However, to return to Philiphaugh in 1983. I was tackled into touch, and out of the tournament, by Bob Hogarth. I damaged a hand and my left shoulder but it was the shoulder, which was causing the most bother. As my jersey was yanked off in the changing room the AC joint popped out. The Good Samaritan who did the yanking was none other than the former international referee Brian Anderson who just happened to be passing the open dressing-room door and who saw me struggling. So, I had gone from being super-fit to the injured list in a single moment. Four weeks later I had got myself back to a level of fitness that I was really happy with and, in a warm-up game for the Polytechnic against Novocastrians, I went to kick a ball out of play, my leg locked and I did a somersault. That was me under the surgeon's knife for an operation on the right knee cartilage. Suddenly I was out of the picture for a further six weeks. Luckily the surgeon who did the business had loads of experience with sporting cartilage injuries due to his work with the Newcastle United football team and he did a good job.

These were, though, two salutary lessons which take on even more significance in this professional era. Players should appreciate now, more than ever, that they are only a second away from a career-threatening injury. One minute you might be a rugby pro earning decent money and the next you could be injured and unemployed. Young players coming into the game with a view to making a real go of it and turning professional should always endeavour to have a second string to their bow. Try to get some kind of professional or trade qualifications that will stand you in good stead when your rugby career is over, especially, in the event of a serious injury, when that career comes to an end faster than you might have thought.

By the November, though, I had broken through into the Northumberland senior side. I was still only 18 and playing against the likes of Surrey who were fielding Paul Ackford, that great seven-a-side exponent Nick Preston of Richmond, the Harlequin Andy Woodhouse, Francis Emeruawa, the flanker who was one of the brightest up-and-coming stars in English rugby before he got injured, and Marcus Rose, the Rosslyn Park full-back.

Sandy McRae played at full-back for us and I was on the right wing. We also had Richard Breakey, Colin White, the Gosforth prop who found everlasting fame when he drank aftershave at a banquet after a France v England game, Steve Bainbridge, the irascible Gosforth lock, and a number 8 called Giles Smallwood who was the great white hope of Northumberland rugby. He was a British

Universities player who never quite made it but, all in all, I was mixing in some pretty exalted company.

Nevertheless, my ultimate goal was a Scotland cap and I was always very conscious of the fact that, down there in England, it might have been a case of out of sight, out of mind. Alistair Tait, who was just then beginning to break through into the Kelso side, was getting rave reviews for his performances in the centre and, from very early on, I had earmarked him as one of my chief rivals for international honours. And this despite the fact that I had yet to make any real impact at centre. Until I was well on into my senior career I was most often looked upon as a wing or a full-back.

I hoped that my breakthrough into English county rugby meant that some of my exploits were filtering their way back to those who mattered in Scotland.

Just a few days after my 18th birthday, I was selected to play for the Anglo-Scots in the Inter-District Championship against South of Scotland. There wasn't much in the way of organisation in those days. We met up about an hour and a half before the game and had the briefest of chats about what we were going to do. Mike Biggar was also playing for the Anglos that day. You get some indication of how far I had gone in such a short space of time when you realise that just a few years before that I had been one of the hundreds of youngsters running on to the Murrayfield pitch when I distinctly remember tapping Mike on the back of his bald head and saying well done.

I picked up the programme in the dressing-room before the game and there, in the South side, were all those legends. Colin Deans, Roy Laidlaw, Jim Aitken, Peter Dods, Iwan Tukalo, John Jeffrey, Iain Paxton, Roger Baird. They were all heroes of mine and there I was supposed to be playing against them. Maybe it all got to me but I had a terrible game. I was still kicking for the Anglos in those days and nothing went right. That was a real eye-opener for me. Until then it had all been relatively easy but that game really brought it home to me that it wasn't going to be an easy haul, and if I was still determined to pursue my goal of a Scottish cap then it was going to be a great deal harder than I had imagined.

I was carrying an injury for the next championship game, against North and Midlands, and had to pull out of the side. Ian McGeechan, who was coaching us, had to pull on his boots and take

over from me at fly-half and that match at Dunfermline marked
Geech's retirement from the playing side.

Even though I had played badly against the South and progress
toward my Scotland cap goal might have been affected as a result, I
refused to let it get me down. I'm an eternal optimist. I always see
the bottle half full rather than half empty. I suppose I've been blessed
with the ability to put set-backs behind me almost immediately.
Even in the context of a single game when things have been going
badly or when, maybe, I've made a bit of a botch of something, I
forget it immediately. It's done, it's in the past, and nothing can
change it. You still, though, have the opportunity to improve on
your performance and make things better. If things haven't been
going well you can still pull off the best tackle, the best try, the best
pass. You can still salvage something from even the worst of games.

We were pretty comprehensively thrashed by the South that day
and, I recall, the game was cut short due to a neck injury to Mike
Biggar. Perhaps I hadn't done myself justice but being selected for the
Anglo-Scots had proved to me that I hadn't been forgotten and that
I wasn't out of the race towards the Scotland side. Despite the fact
that the inter-district championship has taken a great deal of stick in
many quarters I still believe that it performs a worthwhile service,
and especially so for English-based players, because it lets them show
what they can do on the Scottish representative stage.

How much longer this can continue to be the case, with English
players tied to club contracts, remains to be seen but I know that
when I was in Newcastle I was grateful for the opportunity to display
my wares before the Scottish selectors through the medium of the
district championship. It has represented a safety net for players who
would otherwise have disappeared from the Scottish scene. I think
the myth should be quashed, too, that Anglos – or Exiles, as they are
now termed – aren't as motivated when they finally get to pull on
that blue Scotland shirt as home-based players.

That's nonsense. Playing alongside Ian Smith the Gloucester
flanker, you very quickly appreciate that he is just as motivated and
just as proud of the thistle as anybody else in the side. He may betray
his roots with the broadest of West Country dialects but his heart is
in Scotland and that is what counts.

Traditionally, we have so few really class players in Scotland – just
because we are starting from a narrower base than our international

rivals – that we have to spread our net very wide indeed. If the Exiles have Scottish ancestry then there's no reason why they shouldn't play for Scotland. The minimum qualification which renders a player eligible for Scotland selection is the 'possession' of a Scottish grandparent. We don't go for the residential qualifications which are also permissible under International Board regulations. It would be foolish to declare that we should never adopt a policy of qualifying for Scotland through residence because every case should be treated on its individual merits but I'm happy enough with the system we have just now.

My ex-Scotland centre partner Sean Lineen is a prime example of a player who came into the side – and not everyone agreed with it at the time – on the basis of a Hebridean grandparent. But we struck up a great friendship, on and off the field, and there was never any doubt about where Sean's loyalties lay. He was Scottish through and through. I was best man at his wedding to Lynn, and Sean made it clear very early on that he was in Scotland for the long haul and not just as a rugby mercenary wanting to pick up a few cheap caps.

But where I do fall out with the SRU is where they have fast-tracked certain players to the international side. The South African Harry Roberts is a case in point. Roberts, who was just over here for a year, was catapulted to a Scotland B cap at hooker and then disappeared back to South Africa. To a lesser extent, John Allan comes into this category too. Basically, he used Scotland and Scottish representative honours to benefit his career in South Africa. I would like to have seen John stay. He was a good player, even although his inclusion in the Scotland side was dreadfully unfair on Kenny Milne, but he decided to go back home where he went on to play for the Springboks. Somebody whose heart was very firmly within the Scotland camp would never have done that. We have to be very, very careful about who we pick for Scotland.

However, to return to the plot, I was committed to Newcastle and still playing representative rugby with Edinburgh, and Northumberland. A letter arrived from Murrayfield in the spring of 1984 informing me that I had been selected to play for Scotland Under-21 against Combined Services Under-21 at Murrayfield. I had been chosen at centre and my partner was none other than A.V. Tait of Kelso. Alastair had by this time been involved in senior Scotland training sessions. He was a fine player who, of course, went on to play top-grade rugby league after he had got his Scotland caps, and I have to admit that, back in 1984, I was very envious of him indeed. He never made any secret of the fact that he saw his future in rugby league. His father had played professionally and, although I don't suggest that it was quite as cynical as it might sound, there is no doubt that once Ally had got his six Scottish caps, his market value in rugby league terms rose accordingly.

We beat Combined Services pretty convincingly despite the fact that within their ranks they had one Rory Underwood. He was a flyer then just as he is now. He scored a try against us and after the game one of the Combined Services bufties, a Group Captain somebody-or-other, stood up to declare what a wonderful try it had been before adding that he hoped it would be the first of many for Rory at Murrayfield. No chance.

By the end of the season I had finished my college course, got my HND in business studies, and disappeared off to America for a few months as a soccer counsellor at US BUNA Camp. Both Gavin and Graeme had gone off to the States on the same kind of operation. It is a student exchange scheme whereby Americans come over here and we go over there for the summer months. You're basically put on the staff at one of those summer camps which are so beloved of the Americans who send their offspring to the wilderness for 12 weeks in the summer. It's a fantastic opportunity to see America while your board and lodgings are paid, the only slight fly in the ointment being that you have to suffer those little rich kids for that part of your stay when you are actually on camp duty.

I was a counsellor at Camp Wah-nee, Torrington, Connecticut. I was to teach the kids soccer. The camp manager – should that be commandant? – was interested in rugby but once I started to explain the laws to him he glazed over and declared that he couldn't really see it catching on. Nevertheless, I had a great time. We were coaching kids aged from six to 16 and would take them away to play in tournaments against rival camps. Again the world of rugby turned out to be a very small one. While I was at Camp Wah-nee I bumped into an Australian, Paul 'Wally' Collins, who represented Australian Schools as a tight-head prop and that is another friendship that has been maintained to this day. Similarly, two New Zealand girls who were gymnastic counsellors at camp made a point of getting in touch when I was in NZ with Scotland and the Lions and so the worldwide network of friends and acquaintances just keeps on growing.

Camp Wah-nee had a reputation for being one of the top basketball summer camps and whenever a big game was coming up the basketball side would be out practising from six in the morning. The noise they made meant that you got an unwanted early morning wake-up call so one of the other counsellors and I sneaked out of our hut at the dead of night with a step-ladder and tied up every single basketball net. We got into a bit of trouble for that but at least we got one long lie-in from our nocturnal endeavours.

The camps are run along military lines with parades and flag ceremonies every morning. Most of the 'inmates' come from rich families where, maybe, both parents work and camp provides an answer to the problem of what to do with the youngsters during the long summer vacation. I have to admit that the concept of packing off your kids to the regimented summer camp life for ten or eleven weeks every year is one which is alien to me but it's part of the great American tradition and who am I to pass judgement?

After the official part of my American trip was over I still had six weeks left on my visa and so took the opportunity to see as much of the States as I could. It was a marvellous experience and I'd certainly recommend it to any student who is looking for meaningful and rewarding summer work away from home.

All good things, though, come to an end and too soon it was time to return to Scotland and think about getting a job. I wasn't long back in Edinburgh before a letter arrived from the Charles Barker advertising agency. They were offering me a job as a 'traffic manager' and I started with them in the December of 1985. I had also returned to Watsonians and was playing my rugby at Myreside once again so things were going along just superbly. We went five games undefeated in the league in the first of which, against Jed-Forest, I scored a hat-trick of tries while playing on the wing. The chairman of Scotland selectors, Robin Charters, was in the crowd and I don't know whether he put in a word for me or not but, within a couple of weeks, things just started getting better and better when I got the call-up for my first national squad session still aged just 20.

Once again, I couldn't quite believe that it was all happening so quickly. There I was part of the Scotland squad and training alongside most of the guys who had won the 1984 Grand Slam. Then it got better still. Gavin, who was the B team full-back – there wasn't an A team at this time – was away playing for Cambridge University. The Scotland B game against Italy clashed with the Varsity match and I was called into the side in his place. Thanks Gav. I played reasonably well under atrocious conditions at Old Anniesland and we won 9–0. By now I was also a regular in the senior Edinburgh district side and that season we won a district championship Grand Slam.

Suddenly, my career just seemed to have accelerated out of all recognition to how it had been just 12 months before. There were five Watsonians in the squad – Gavin and me plus David and Stuart Johnston, and the flanker Clive Millar – so it was being recognised at national level that we were playing some pretty impressive rugby at Myreside.

At that point I was still being looked upon as a utility player. I had played representative and senior club rugby at stand-off, centre, wing and full-back. Even I didn't know what my best position was but, with Euan Kennedy and David Johnston playing in the centre for Watsonians and with Gavin being away at Cambridge, I was reckoned at Myreside, at least, to be first and foremost a full-back.

My first experience of the national set-up took place on the Murrayfield back-pitch on a rain-lashed Wednesday night. Ian McGeechan was in charge of the backs and, strange though it now seems, some of the things that he was getting us to do were completely alien to us. He was drumming into us how he wanted the three quarters to run straight and was instructing us to adopt a staggered start technique which meant that at centre you didn't start moving until the fly-half had moved and the outside centre didn't move until the inside man was off his blocks. All very interesting and, really, the very beginning of the style which would take us through to the Grand Slam in 1990.

I thought I was going places but, in one of those revealing incidents that really put you in your place, I realised that I still had a bit to do. When I had originally been called into the Scotland squad I thought I had made it but then, after the track suits had been handed out, I was given a big white 'B' to sew on beneath the thistle. I sewed the B on to the blue track suit, all the while thinking that the dratted letter would be back off again pretty damn quickly if I could do anything about it. And the opportunity to do just that arrived far sooner than even I – the eternal optimist – could ever have imagined.

4

Christmas Comes Early

CENTRE OF ATTRACTION

CHRISTMAS 1985 was an amazing time for me. I had started a new job. I had won my first B cap and was a member of the Scotland squad. What next? Well, it had to be a place in the international trial which, traditionally, took place just after the New Year.

Despite the fact that I seemed to be throwing double-six with every roll of the dice I was by no means sure that I would get an outing in the trial. For one thing — and perhaps this was most important of all — I wasn't sure just where the selectors thought my future lay. Euan Kennedy, David Johnston, Keith Robertson, Simon Scott of Stewart's Melville, Alan Tait, Iwan Tukalo, Peter Dods and Keith Murray of Hawick all seemed to be ahead of me in the pecking order. I had played one game at centre for Edinburgh against South of Scotland in the district championship and had out-played Murray, so there was a possibility that I might get in, somewhere, ahead of him at least.

Then the letter came telling me that I had been picked to play at centre for the junior Reds side alongside Simon Scott against David Johnston and Keith Robertson. This was only my third or fourth game at centre and so you can appreciate how apprehensive I was and especially because I was in direct opposition to David Johnston who was, in my opinion, one of the best footballers — in the sense of being a gifted and cultured all-rounder — that Scottish rugby has ever produced. He was a great thinking player. He thought very deeply about the game and this was reflected in his subsequent elevation to coach the Scotland A side and, then, to become backs' coach with the full international side.

So, selection for the trial represented, for me, an extremely long shot. That Reds team, though, contained a lot of players who were knocking on the door and desperate to prove their worth: Gavin Hastings, Stuart McAuslan, Simon Scott, me, Roger Baird, Doug Wyllie, Stuart Johnston, David Sole, Garry Callander, Norrie Rowan, Alister Campbell, Jeremy Campbell-Lamerton, Derek White, John Beattie and Fin Calder.

We had a pretty strong pack led by Gary Callander, the Kelso hooker who had deputised so many times for Colin Deans, and he had a real point to prove. The Blues' side at Murrayfield that day was Peter Dods, Matt Duncan, Keith Robertson, David Johnston, Iwan Tukalo, John Rutherford, Roy Laidlaw, Alex Brewster, Colin Deans, Iain Milne, Hugh Parker, Alan Tomes, Jim Calder, Iain Paxton and John Jeffrey.

That trial match, which we won 41–10, has entered Scottish rugby folklore. We absolutely hammered the Blues. Maybe the selectors couldn't quite believe what they were seeing because they asked for an extra ten minutes to be played. Trials can be the most awkward of games. In recent seasons the SRU have more or less abandoned the concept because of the amount of representative rugby being played. From the comfort of my position as a senior player – although the comfort is only relative because no matter how many caps you have you're still only as good as your last game – I can say that I entirely agree with that decision. However, I'm mindful of the fact that if we young guns hadn't been given the opportunity to play a trial match then it was a moot-point as to whether the selectors would have had the courage to make quite so many changes as they eventually did.

Almost certainly the only guy who can lose out from a trial is the sitting tenant. The bloke knocking on the door has everything to win and nothing to lose. The man in possession is just playing to retain what he's already got. You can imagine, therefore, why trial games are not particularly popular with the Society of Sitting Tenants. However, nobody has a God-given right to become a permanent fixture in the Scottish rugby team – as I was to find to my cost in later years – and on 4 January 1986 at Murrayfield we resolved to stake our claims for the national side, one month after my 21st birthday.

At that time there was even more to play for than usual. Scotland had won the Grand Slam in 1984 and had gone from that pinnacle of achievement to a wooden spoon in the very next season. Maybe a few of the Grand Slam heroes were reaching their sell-by dates. The Reds knew that and we went at them hell for leather. Stuart Johnston, my Watsonian clubmate who was the Reds' scrum-half, was really the catalyst for much of our success and it remains one of my great sadnesses that, of us all, Stuart probably produced the best individual performance but lost out when the Scotland side was picked.

I have always prided myself on my level of fitness but I was absolutely shattered after that trial. I went home, had a mug of tea and went straight to bed. I had agreed to meet Stuart Johnston for a beer later and when we arrived at the King's Bar in Bruntsfield the afternoon's events at Murrayfield was the sole topic of conversation. The result really did send shockwaves through the game. The big debate was on in the bar: who was going to get the axe and who was going to get in. Some said I'd be in and others said Stuart was a certainty but to get his cap he would have to get the nod over Roy Laidlaw. To get in at centre I would have to leap-frog Keith Robertson, Doug Wyllie, David Johnston, Keith Murray or big Euan Kennedy. Was that likely? Only the selectors knew and they wouldn't be telling for another three days.

The next day, a Sunday, we were back at Murrayfield for a squad session. In those days the sessions could go on for anything between two and three hours. Near the end of the session, with the team still unannounced, we went through a few backs' moves and I was slotted in alongside Roy Laidlaw, John Rutherford, David Johnston, Matt Duncan and Roger Baird. Peter Dods was at full-back but Gavin had injured an eye in the trial so couldn't take part in the session. Hello, I thought. What does this mean? Gavin couldn't drive because of the injury to his eye but dad brought him down to the session just as it was ending and he came out into the main stadium and saw me lining up in what appeared to be a prospective Scotland back division. Because of his injury he didn't have the comfort, wrong though it might have been if I had been reading something into it that wasn't there, of knowing that at least I seemed to be in with a shout. The selectors were picking the team on the Monday night but we wouldn't know the results of their deliberations until the Wednesday. That was a long couple of days.

Because I had just started a new job the month before I was keen not to be late for work but equally keen to catch the postman arriving at about 8.45 a.m. I decided to risk a telling-off at work and wait for the postie. When the letter arrived I ripped it open and read it more in disbelief than anything. I was in. Absolutely fantastic. The first person I told was Jenny, then my girlfriend and now my wife. After I had telephoned her I went through to see mum in the next room. She had sneaked a bottle of champagne into the fridge in case one of us got into the side. The feeling, I think, was that Scott had played a good trial but he was still only 21 and the major recipient of the champers would be Gavin.

The fact that two brown envelopes had appeared meant that it had been looking hopeful for both of us and we would both be celebrating. The SRU have rather spoiled the surprise element of these brown envelopes nowadays because they now have your number written on the front. You know before you open them whether you are in the team or whether you are going to be a replacement.

Once I'd broken the news to mum I climbed the stairs to Gavin's room. He was back from Cambridge and I said to him: 'Are you in?'

He said: 'Yup.'

I said: 'So am I.'

And that was it. It was the most simple of exchanges. Really downbeat. We agreed that we'd have a few beers after work and I went back downstairs to tell mum that Gavin was in as well, and there she was in tears.

She was reading an article in the newspaper about Richard Cross, a 28-year-old London Irish full-back, who had died after breaking his neck in a reserve game against London Scottish. He had left a wife and an 18-month-old son and, probably with the mixed emotions of her sons being selected for Scotland and reading that tragic story in the paper, mum was quite overcome.

As we all know now there were six new caps in the side. Gavin and I, Fin Calder, Matt Duncan, David Sole and Jeremy Campbell-Lamerton were the new faces in the side to meet France in just ten days' time. I went off to work feeling on top of the world and the first person I bumped into was Simon Scott, who was an accountant with the same firm.

He asked me if I had got a letter. I said I had and he said he hadn't.

He went off to his desk and made a few phone calls, only to find out that David Johnston was the other centre and there wasn't a place for him. Simon had set me up for a superb try in the trial and it was difficult not to feel for him because although he got on to the bench when we went to Romania later that season, this was as close as Simon got to a cap and, on his performance in the trial, he deserved one as much as anybody. We had to travel through to a meeting in Glasgow together later that day and Simon even took me out for lunch, despite the fact that he must have been feeling pretty pissed off with life.

The media interest in the six new caps and the fact that two brothers had been selected to make their debuts together was just amazing. The phone never stopped ringing and there were TV crews clamouring for interviews with Gavin and I. After work, family and friends began arriving at the house. It was great for our parents. They had given us so much support in our rugby careers and now both of us were to be capped on the same day. Brothers had, of course, played together for Scotland before but I don't think that brothers had ever been picked to make their debuts on the same day.

We now had a long wait for the game. I wrapped myself in cotton wool and made myself unavailable for Watsonians' game against Kilmarnock the following weekend and was glad that I'd done so. It was played in the most atrocious conditions and the Kilmarnock full-back was taken off with hypothermia.

I had played just a handful of games at centre and for my international debut I would be marking Philippe Sell,a who was one of the all-time greats. That was daunting enough but when I went to Murrayfield for the squad session on the Sunday before the big game the most remarkable incident occurred which, if I had been of a timid disposition, would have wrecked my confidence entirely.

I was walking from the dressing-room out on to the pitch to have my photograph taken for the programme, when I bumped into Ian MacGregor, the chairman of selectors. He is a notoriously gruff individual and without so much as a by-your-leave he stopped me in the tunnel and growled: 'Just remember one thing. You didn't get my fucking vote.'

I was absolutely stunned and just stammered: 'What?'

'You didn't get my fucking vote, son. And don't you forget it,' he repeated.

I couldn't believe it. Here was the chairman of selectors, six days before an important Test match and the biggest game of my life, telling me that he didn't want me in the side. I've never been able to fathom the guy out. I don't know why he did it and I've never raised it with him since but it left a marked impression on me. I had to brush it aside and just pretend to myself that it had never happened. I didn't really mention it to any of my team-mates but they could see that something had upset me. From that day onwards I decided that I would just play my own game, do my best and if it wasn't good enough then so be it.

The team which the selectors picked to represent Scotland against France at Murrayfield on Saturday, 18 January 1986, read: Gavin Hastings, Matt Duncan, David Johnston, Scott Hastings, Roger Baird, John Rutherford, Roy Laidlaw, David Sole, Colin Deans, Iain Milne, Alister Campbell, Jeremy Campbell-Lamerton, John Jeffrey, John Beattie and Finlay Calder. It was new caps for me and Gavin, Matt, David, Fin and Jeremy. We were the first brothers to make our international debuts together this century and, for us, the build-up to the game was just immense.

Until recently I didn't get nervous before games. You begin to feel the adrenalin kicking in two or three days before the kick-off and it is the adrenalin that carries me through. Gavin, of course, was still at home which meant that the only topic of conversation was The Game. What were we going to do? How were we going to play it. There was apprehension certainly but, generally, just a great sense of expectation.

The team got together for a Murrayfield practice on the Thursday before the game and then it would be off to the Braid Hills Hotel in Edinburgh which would be our base for the weekend. We no longer stay there but for years it had been Scotland's traditional team hotel, and on my first visit it didn't take me long to find out why.

It seems incredible now, in these days when we are all given finely-tuned diet sheets and told what to eat and when, but, back in 1986, staying at the Braid Hills was like giving a foodaholic the keys to the kitchen. We stuffed ourselves with massive three-course meals – the biggest bowl of vegetable soup you could lay your hands on followed by sole goujon and a sirloin steak the size of Texas. Meal times would be a gastronomic delight, always followed by a couple of hours when you would just put the feet up. A real sumo wrestler's diet! The senior players would disappear off to the bar for a few beers and, to be honest, it was a fairly relaxed atmosphere.

On the Friday before the game we had the Press session at Murrayfield when, again, Gavin and I were centres of attention. 'Where are the Hasteengs brothers?' the French journalists would ask. I was totally relaxed. Colin Deans, in his autobiography, recalls how he was prowling around the hotel like a caged lion whereas Gavin and I were laid back to the point of nonchalance. I even asked him at one point if he could fetch me a cup of tea! There was Deans, captain of Scotland with 39 caps, and me with none asking him to run an errand. But it wasn't an act. I was just savouring the whole experience and was totally without nerves.

Everything had happened so quickly for me and I was being carried along on the crest of a wave. Finally I had all of my Scotland kit without the dreaded 'B' under the thistle and I could not have been happier. Friday night, again in line with tradition, meant a visit to the Dominion cinema and I slept as sound as a log on the eve of the biggest game of my life.

Nowadays, I have to admit that I do begin to tense up a bit by the Saturday lunch-time but that's because I now know just how bloody difficult international rugby can be. Back then I just took each moment of each day as it came and savoured that moment as deeply as I could.

Nerves generally don't bother me, as I say, but that doesn't mean that I'm unaware of the honour and responsibility which representing your country brings with it. You are a member of a 15-man team and – despite what Ian MacGregor might have thought – each of you is the best in his position in the whole country. That, at least, is the theory and there is no room for self-doubt in a Test match. You are representing all Scots everywhere, and their hopes and aspirations rest on your shoulders. You are also aware of all those Scottish internationalists who have preceded you and also that, as you play, you are creating your team's little bit of history. On a more down-to-earth level you are representing your family and your club and your friends. Generally, the opportunity to represent your country comes only four or five times in a season so the very rarity of the prize makes it all the more worth winning.

Before my first Test, as I have done before all the others, I try to construct a mental picture of what is going to happen and how I am going to react to the 1001 incidents that can occur in an international match. As we shall see there was one incident in particular that played no part in my mental movie, but more of that later. My immediate opponent was going to be Philippe Sella who was winning his 24th cap. Gavin's opposite number was Serge Blanco, one of the greatest full-backs of all time, who already had 33 caps to his name. The French side oozed experience and here were Scotland with six virgin soldiers in the front line.

Frankly, I knew next to nothing about the Tricolours. I had watched them as a schoolboy at Murrayfield and knew that from a backs' perspective they could be absolutely lethal but, in detail, I knew zilch. There has always been something different about the French. There is an athleticism about them which the other Five Nations partners don't always have. They even handle the ball differently. There's a crispness and a sweetness to their passing technique which is almost unique to them.

With the game almost upon us David Johnston took me aside for some last-minute words of wisdom. 'Remember,' he said, 'when you run out on to Murrayfield you are there to do a job. Don't get lost in the crowd. Don't go rubber-necking to see your family and your friends in the stand. Forget them. You can see them any time. You've been picked to play rugby for Scotland and that, and only that is what you are at Murrayfield to do.'

That was the second spot of advice I'd received from a Watsonian colleague. During the week before the game, a letter arrived from Euan Kennedy. There were the usual congratulations and good-lucks but then Euan went on to write about the Murrayfield tunnel. In the old West Stand it was about 30 yards long, a dour, dank place with brown gloss paint on the walls and a black rubber carpet on the concrete floor to protect the boot studs. For all the world it looked like a tenement close.

You would emerge from the brightly lit changing-room at the rear of the stand into this badly lit, smelly passageway. Turn right, left and right again and there you were at the tunnel with daylight beckoning you towards the stadium at the end. Euan wrote about coming out of the darkness into the light literally at the end of the tunnel, and of the welcome that you could expect as the crowd caught its first glimpse of you. Like me, he said, he had dreamt of running out of that tunnel on to the Murrayfield turf and, he added, there was nothing to compare with it. He was right. To win your first cap at Murrayfield, where you had stood as a boy, is just an incredible experience and it is one that you will take with you to the grave.

That was the moment that I focused upon as the game drew near. That was when you really won your first cap. It wasn't when you got the letter. You still had to avoid injury; still had to avoid getting knocked over by the bus at the end of the road. You had won your cap when you ran out on to the pitch.

The dressing-room just before an international match is not a place for the faint-hearted. There are those who bawl and shout and others who sit quietly. The Hawick lock 'Sally' Campbell was someone who was always troubled by his stomach. Roy Laidlaw would be sitting quietly in a corner, Johnny Beattie would be putting on a pretty convincing one-man performance of the Texas Chain Saw Massacre and 'Sally' would be through in the loo bringing up his breakfast.

Our introduction to international rugby was straight out of Fred Karno's Circus. The game was just 20 seconds old and Pierre Berbizier had run in for a try which gave France a four-point lead. What the hell had happened? Gavin had kicked off and, with his first touch in international rugby, the ball had flown straight into touch. Normally, the opposition would have opted for a scrummage at the centre-spot and this was what we all assumed was going to happen. Berbizier had other ideas. He took the throw-in to himself and ran from the half-way line for the try. They never said international rugby was going to be like this. When we were behind our line waiting for the conversion attempt I turned to Johnny Beattie and asked him what was going on.

'Search me,' he said. Or words to that effect. Well, if he hadn't a clue with his 30-odd caps for Scotland, then what chance was there for the rest of us? Guy Laporte missed the kick at goal and, once we had gathered our senses, we just told ourselves to put it behind us.

Soon after, Gavin had his first crack at a penalty goal. He put it over and, suddenly, we were right back in the game. Very early on John Rutherford turned to me and said that I was to put up a high ball on Blanco. It was an absolute peach and served as a real confidence booster for me. The entire Scotland pack pounced on Blanco and gave him a right good rucking. It was that kind of touch by Rutherford which meant so much to the new boys. He had decided early on that he wanted to bring me into the game. Because I had done what he wanted correctly, that acted as a calming influence and set me up for the game.

It's now part of Scottish rugby lore, of course, that we won that day 18–17 and that Gavin kicked all of Scotland's points. I was pleased with the way that my debut had gone as well. I had tackled everything that moved and, although I do say it myself, had got the better of Sella. At the final whistle I ran towards Gavin and we walked off the pitch arm in arm. It was only at that point that we had a chance to discuss what had happened at the kick-off. Gavin, typically, was completely unfazed by it all. He had set a new Scottish Five Nations points record and we had won. What a start. The celebrations began right away in the dressing-room when quite a few beers were consumed, and by the time we got to the SRU president's reception in the Carlton Highland Hotel some of us were half cut. Changed days.

It was high jinks, too, at the dinner, at which what became known as the 'stuffed tomato incident' occurred in all of its juicy glory. To this day Gavin denies it, but I was a witness and my lips can remain sealed no longer. The facts, m'lud are these. A stuffed tomato emerged from the ranks of the Scottish players and struck a senior executive of match sponsors the Royal Bank of Scotland square on the front of his best bib and tucker. Outrage. Who could have committed such a heinous felony and one which led to a communal tongue-lashing from the SRU president a fortnight later as we got ready to play Wales? I cannot tell a lie and, however much he might seek to deny it, the culprit was Gavin, m'lud. I saw him commit the deed with my own two eyes. There has been a wicked suggestion in the intervening period that I was the phantom tomato chucker. Well, it's not the first time in our lives that I have ended up carrying the can for a Gavin misdemeanour but on this occasion, I swear, Gavin had taken far, far too much to drink in celebration of his six penalty goals and it was him wot dunnit. There rests the case for the defence. In those days after-match dinners were a bit of a good-natured rabble. Behaviour is much better nowadays. However, many of the pranks which went on were merely a safety valve for the pressure built up during the previous three full days of commitment to the national cause.

Meanwhile, back at 18 Merchiston Place, our folks were also having a hell of a party. Some friends from Newcastle Northern had travelled up to watch me making my debut, and a few stray Frenchmen had ended up in the house. It was all going like a fair. There was still plenty of champagne left when Gavin and I made it home on the Sunday and the most fantastic weekend of our lives was at an end.

Next, though, we had to wait to see whether we were going to be selected again for the game against Wales in Cardiff. We were pretty confident. Nothing much had gone wrong and, of course, Gavin had kicked himself into the record books. All of the six new caps, with the exception of the desperately unfortunate Jeremy Campbell-Lamerton, were back in the side. The vastly experienced Iain Paxton had recovered from injury in time for Cardiff and Jeremy's place went to him. The dropping of Jeremy served as a reminder to us all, I think, that you could take absolutely nothing for granted and really had to play for your place every time you pulled on that Scotland jersey.

Cardiff Arms Park, that great shrine to Welsh rugby, held no terrors for me. Watching the Five Nations' games on TV and listening to the massed choirs singing in Cardiff had always sent a tingle down my spine and, far from being intimidated by it, I reckoned that I could get a lift just as invigorating from it as the Welsh players. We stayed at the St Pierre Hotel and Country Club in Chepstow, as we still do, and I was sharing a room with John Rutherford. On the Friday night before the game I was awakened in the wee small hours by Rudd pacing around the room.

'Get back to sleep, Scott. There's no point in you being awake as well,' he said. Even with all his caps and all his experience he was as nervous as a kitten. Again, I was completely at ease. It was all new to me. I'd never been in Chepstow. I had never been to Cardiff and it was all part of an unbelievable dream come true.

But there was no story-book ending in Wales. After an amazing game of rugby, in which the Welsh wizard Jonathan Davies showed us all his tricks, we lost 22–15. It was a good Welsh team and, probably, they deserved their victory. But the game will be recalled most of all for the record-breaking penalty goal by Paul Thorburn. The kick has been measured as being from 12 metres inside the Welsh half so the distance was at least 62 metres, and more when the angle is taken into account. Finlay Calder had given away a late-tackle penalty on Jonathan Davies just outside the Welsh 22. Jonathan's kick hadn't gone far and the referee gave the penalty from where, as Bill McLaren says, the ball alighted. We couldn't quite believe it when Thorburn opted to go for goal but he struck it well and the ball just kept on going and going and going. What a sickener.

I expected us to win and took defeat rather badly. I couldn't quite believe the unspoken feeling within the Scottish camp that because we were playing away from home we were almost expected to lose. Call me naïve, but every time I step on to a rugby field I genuinely believe that we are going to win. There's a corrosive mind-set in all of this and if you start a Five Nations' season thinking that you'll win your home games and, just maybe, you'll win the away games then you're never going to get anywhere.

Nevertheless, disappointment in Cardiff was compensated for to some degree by our victory over England a fortnight later by the immensely satisfying and record margin of 33–6. Because of snow and frost, that Calcutta Cup game was one of the few sporting events which went on that weekend. We had travelled down to North Berwick to get a frost-free, sea side pitch on which to train, the week before, but the weather never relented and two days prior to the game, we did some work at Easter Road, the home of Hibernian FC. The fixture was saved by the Murrayfield blanket operating at full blast and thank goodness it worked.

We led 12–6 at half-time, Gavin again being on superlative kicking form, but in the second half we really cut loose and handled the ball superbly well. We got tries from Matt Duncan, John Rutherford and me – my first for Scotland. Gavin kicked all the conversions plus another penalty for a 100 per cent goal-kicking record.

It's a special moment to score your first try for your country. We had been capitalising on English mistakes, aided by the New Zealand referee Bob Francis who had a real feel for the game and let it flow splendidly well. Roger Baird picked up a spilled England pass and started counter-attacking. At the time I was well back on the 22. The ball came back to John Rutherford via Johnny Beattie and Roy Laidlaw. By the time I got the ball there wasn't an Englishman in sight and, after a wee bit of juggling, I sprinted in to touch down under the posts. Gavin stepped forward to steer home the conversion and we had logged a record defeat against the Auld Enemy.

When I was a primary five pupil at George Watson's College, the Calcutta Cup had, for some reason or other, been brought to the school. I had held it as a ten-year-old and here I was at the dinner after the game back in the proximity of the trophy which I was utterly enchanted by.

So much so, that now I can exclusively reveal – as they say in the very best journalistic circles – that I took the lovely ornate silver trophy for an unauthorised jaunt on to the streets of Edinburgh two full years before the celebrated episode involving allegedly – again as they say in journalistic circles – John Jeffrey and Dean Richards. It was full to the brim with whisky and many was the toast which was drunk on Edinburgh's North Bridge outside the hotel in which the dinner was being held.

I must say I took much better care of the cup than was the case in 1988 and, after half an hour or so, a SRU official appeared on the scene to suggest that it might be a good idea if the cup and I returned to the sanctity of the dinner. We did so via the main bar in the hotel and, after an hour, the cup was back on its pedestal and I was off to my bed in disgrace having indulged much too enthusiastically in after-dinner refreshment.

After three games we topped the championship table on points difference and next on the agenda was Ireland in Dublin. I have always found tussles with the Irish at Lansdowne Road much more difficult than I should. The ground itself is odd. There are two quaint pavilions looking very much out of place in a stadium setting. A railway line runs under one of the stands and there's this strange terracing which just looks as if it shouldn't be there at all.

The eccentricity of the architecture is more than matched by the quaintness of the Irish crowd, which is so fickle that it can turn on its team if things aren't going their way. Conversely they can also make the most incredible amount of noise when their side has got its tail up. It's a funny old town Dublin, and I found my first visit there quite disconcerting.

We won 10–9 but that game is remembered most by me for the fact that it was the first time in a Scotland shirt that I had missed a tackle. Trevor Ringland, the Irish right winger, ran past me and then, with 10 minutes to go, I took a short pass off John Rutherford, mishandled, and the ball bounced straight to Tony Ward. Suddenly they were 60 metres upfield whereas if I had held the pass we would, perhaps, have scored and put the issue beyond any doubt.

I reckoned that these were the first mistakes I had made while playing for Scotland and I came off the pitch feeling very disillusioned. Strangely, ever since then I have always been just that little bit more apprehensive before a Lansdowne Road game than at any other venue where I've played international rugby. It's funny how these things prey on your mind. As I've said, I always try to look on the bright side, and I do find it disconcerting that Lansdowne Road, for me, is always associated with my first mistakes in Test rugby.

So, that was the championship season over. We finished joint top of the Five Nations table with France. It was a brilliant result considering that we had such a new-look side.

The Five Nations' tournament was done and dusted but the season itself was not yet finished. We still had to travel to pre-revolution Bucharest to take on Romania in the ever so-romantically named 23 August Stadium.

It was grim. We were berthed in the city-centre Intercontinental Hotel. They didn't have any food to serve us and if you asked for the dining-room lights to be turned up then they went off in the rest of the hotel. The SRU had the foresight to take over our own food but most of it disappeared when we got over there. The country really was in a shocking condition. The streets were dirty. The people had a dreadful downtrodden look about them and it came as no surprise when Ceaucescu and his comrades were toppled from power just four years later.

It was a unique experience for me. I had never seen deprivation like this before. During our stay, I had to call a plumber to the hotel room I was sharing, again with John Rutherford, and this guy ended up pleading with us to give him our training shoes. Every time we left the hotel – not that we did often – we were followed around the grey, bleak streets by the Securetate secret police. After the game, which we won 33–18 and during which I scored my second international try, a couple of the Romanian players came back to the city centre in our bus. We had a whip-round in US dollars so that they and their team-mates could have some fun. Fun, like everything else, was strictly rationed in Ceaucescu's Romania.

The post-match banquet consisted of bread, lettuce and something which we couldn't quite put a name to so we left it alone. Sadly, there was a plentiful supply of Romanian wine. The upshot was that most of us drank too much on empty stomachs and when we got back to the hotel there was a certain amount of damage done to fixtures and fittings.

A bed was broken, a lamp was knocked over and, most seriously of all, a bedroom door became decidedly second-hand. The next morning the hotel authorities presented us with a bill for damage which they said amounted to £1,000. I will not deny for a second that some damage had been done and – older and wiser that I am – I admit that was regrettable. However, there was no way on earth that it was going to cost £1,000 to put right but we were virtually held to ransom until the cash was found. And by the way, Colin Deans in his autobiography, where he recounts this tale, refers to his hotel door having been made out of balsa wood. Well, Colin, when the Melrose hooker George Runciman and I put our shoulders to your door it sure didn't feel like balsa wood to us!

I'm rather ashamed to admit that when I was 21 and a bit of a blithe spirit I always seemed to be getting myself involved in incidents like that. There was another occasion, after an Ireland game, when I was invited into the ladies' dinner and, through no fault of my own, became the star attraction. I was, of course, wearing the kilt. One thing led to another and soon I was on top of a table trying, but failing, to counter demands to see what a true Scot wears under his highland dress.

I don't know what the ladies thought but the Scottish and Irish rugby unions were distinctly unimpressed and I had to fire off a letter of apology to the IRFU. My defence is that I was always led astray by bigger boys – and on that occasion girls. I was, though, living the life of an international rugby player to the full. It was what I had dreamt of since I was a youngster and it was everything that I had anticipated. My appetite had been well and truly whetted and I couldn't wait for more.

5

Grand Slams and the Auld Enemy

Don't Look Back

THE 1990 Grand Slam was, undoubtedly, the highlight of my career so far and one of the greatest days in the history of the Scottish game, but I wonder if we are not now in danger of feasting too much on past glories. The events of 17 March 1990 were, indeed, glorious. They were heroic and historic and it was marvellous to have been involved but the key word here is 'historic'. We have not beaten England since then and I have been involved in two further Grand Slam encounters with the Auld Enemy, both of which went England's way.

At the time of writing we have beaten England just twice since I won my first cap in 1986 and one of those was the record 33–6 victory in that debut season. The record simply isn't good enough. We can dine out on tales of 1990 from now until eternity but until such time as we can defeat England on a regular basis we will never achieve the status that we should be striving for in Europe, and that is to be, consistently, the number one nation.

This is not to diminish our achievement in 1990. It was fantastic and I hold cherished memories of everything that happened that day, but we have to look forward and not dwell in the past, no matter how pleasant that might be.

It could be argued with more than a little truth that English rugby actually derived more benefit from our Grand Slam win than we did. We knew at the time just how shattered the English team and management had been. They really did think that they were coming to Murrayfield for a leisurely jaunt and that the Grand Slam would be theirs just for the asking.

Since then, though, in a blizzard of books and newspaper articles, the English players who were involved have shown just how severely their pride and their psyche were damaged. The result was that they circled the wagons and devised a style of play – crushingly boring and limited but drastically effective – which ensured that they would win the Grand Slam the following year and again in 1992 and 1995. It is a moot-point as to whether we in Scotland would have been content with such startling success if the price to be paid was a style of rugby which left so much to be desired. I would like to think that we wouldn't but winning at the highest level produces a hypnotic effect in which it is very easy, once all the rivals have been vanquished, to convince yourself that the end more than justifies the means.

Nevertheless, after their defeat at Murrayfield in 1990, England set about getting their act together to become the dominant force in Northern Hemisphere rugby and I have to admit that far too often since our Grand Slam encounter we have struggled to compete with England for a full 80 minutes. Sadly, another facet of our tussles with the Auld Enemy in my time has been the fact that so many of them have been downright poor games.

In 1995 we were both going for the Grand Slam at Twickenham. After the game Brian Moore did his bit for sore winners with his outrageous TV observation that Scotland had come just to spoil. I felt that Brian was silly in the extreme, not only for the timing of his comments but also because he was wrong. We played more real rugby than England did that day and I just wonder how well Scotland could play if we had access to England's resources both in terms of numbers to pick from and the often physically superior specimens that they can draft into their packs.

The story of Grand Slam '90 is now so well known and so copiously documented that even those who weren't there must know it chapter and verse. England thought they were coming to lift the Grand Slam, the Championship, the Triple Crown and the Calcutta Cup.

In direct contravention of International Rugby Football Board regulations we got together on the Wednesday, three days before the game. However, as the IB then and now seem to exert no real or significant authority within the game, this did not cause us much concern.

The Wednesday session at Murrayfield, where temporary floodlights had been specially erected, went very well. Barely a pass went down in 45 minutes of concentrated work and, in fact, coach Ian McGeechan called an early halt because we were so fired up that we were in danger of over-cooking the dish.

By this time I had struck up a fantastic relationship with Sean Lineen, my playing partner in the centre. We shared a common outlook on life which was that it wasn't a rehearsal for anything. This was the big picture and you had to enjoy it while it lasted. We enjoyed ourselves off the pitch too and our high spirits sometimes got us into trouble with the SRU. I recall one training session with the Edinburgh District side when Sean had been out beforehand, enjoying himself on the north side of Edinburgh, and I had been doing likewise on the south side. We must have smelt like a couple of breweries.

Sean was an incredibly creative player. Because of his acute awareness, he made space for those around him and this facility of his was to prove crucial in the Scotland strategy which won the big prize.

The day dawned bright and blustery. The backs had rehearsed our moves in the car park of the Braid Hills Hotel and the forwards had gone down to the nearby Braidburn Valley where they had found a stretch of flat ground on which they went through some rucking drills. The forwards' coach, Jim Telfer, now the SRU's director of rugby, always wanted to put the forwards through their paces on the morning of a match and I vividly recall one previous Scotland–England encounter when I had been sharing a room with Kenny Milne. The hooker came back to the hotel with a nasty gash on his leg. Every member of the pack in turn had been asked to lie on the ball and then his colleagues had rucked over the top of him. If this is what they are doing to each other then heaven help the English, I thought.

The game strategy centred primarily around the back row of John Jeffrey, Derek White and Finlay Calder. Because they were a world-class unit, virtually everything that we did began with them. There was a tendency for the midfield to take the ball up and look for second and third phase possession. Under McGeechan at this point in his coaching career, and because of the effectiveness of the back-row unit, there was, to be honest, never much in the way of all-out, free-flowing back play. But we were playing to our strengths and we were playing winning, 15-man rugby with each player accepting responsibility for every facet of play.

When we left the hotel for the twenty minute bus journey to Murrayfield we were as focused on what lay ahead as any team with which I have been involved. Our emotions were on a knife-edge. I was once asked if I had cried after we had won. Well, I cried in the hotel beforehand. I cried in the bus and I cried when we got to Murrayfield. I really let the emotions come through. It works for me and I think that when we played England again for Grand Slams in 1995 and 1996, maybe this was one of the things which counted against us. We just didn't let our emotions flow on those occasions as I certainly had in 1990.

Sadly, my overwrought emotions got the better of me at one point during the game when I became involved in an incident which I now much regret. My opposite number Jeremy Guscott had been caught in the ribs by one of Fin Calder's notorious shoulder charges. Guscott went down hurt and I shouted: 'Get off, you English black bastard!'

The scene resembled one of those 'Time for a quick exit' TV adverts. It seemed to me that, just as the words escaped, the entire Murrayfield crowd had fallen silent. I'm not a racist. I had known Jerry for a long time and for some inexplicable reason the words just slipped out. We had played together with the British Lions in Australia a year previously and got on reasonably well. There was no malice intended but it was an unfortunate thing to have said.

Actually, Guscott never heard my comments at the time and it wasn't until the dinner after the game that Will Carling said to him: 'Jerry, do you know what Scott called you today?'

I said: 'I called you an English black bastard and I'm very, very embarrassed about it. I didn't mean it and I apologise.'

Jerry replied: 'It's OK Scott. I had a better game than you did today anyway.'

So, that was it and nothing more was said about it. However, five years later he cast up the issue in his autobiography. That surprised me. He had never heard the comment, having got wind of it only through the mischievous intervention of Carling. I had apologised and the apology seemed to have been accepted in the spirit in which it was tendered.

Actually, in his book he misquotes me. He maintains that I had called him a 'black bastard', leaving out the word 'English'. Whether that makes it better or worse I don't know but it is an incident which I am not proud of. Neither do I know whether Jerry would have felt better about it had I just called him an English bastard.

Jerry had, indeed, played well. He had opened the scoring for England with a try. He really is a thoroughbred. He has a seemingly effortless, gliding style of running and, despite what some might think, he is also a competent defender. He's a moody individual, though, something which I had discovered with the Lions in Australia. If things weren't going right and if passes were going down in training then he would start getting lippy or he would have a good moan.

England's try came after a fatal defensive error by me. I got sucked in on the wrong side of Will Carling who had made a superb outside break. Once I was out of alignment he handed on to Guscott who dummied Gavin and slipped over for the try. They had taken their chance well but the score had come about through a defensive error and they must have thought that it was all going to be as easy as they had thought beforehand. David Sole brought us around him under the posts and told us that this would be the last tackle missed. It is probably true to say that it was, indeed, the last tackle that any of us missed during an afternoon of high-voltage rugby. I prefer to think that England's opening score came about as a result of a tactical masterstroke by S. Hastings which lulled the English into a false sense of security!

David Sole's leadership during that Grand Slam campaign was significant. The walk on to Murrayfield was a masterstroke which represented an early psychological victory for us. He was never the most charismatic of individuals. Even after all the years that we played together I never got close to him. He was an intensely private person who kept his thoughts very much to himself. His inspirational leadership came from his deeds on the pitch. He led from the front and was, without doubt, one of the very best rugby players, never mind prop forwards, who ever represented Scotland. Technically he was world-class. He was a great handler, an explosive runner and was always to be found where the action was thickest. As a back, I always felt that whenever David took the ball into contact then it was guaranteed that it would come back served up on a plate.

I was surprised when he made the decision to retire from the game so early but he had a young family, had been playing top-grade rugby from a very early age with Bath and, latterly, with Scotland had been involved in a number of unsettling incidents with the SRU hierarchy. As captain of Scotland the demands upon his time were enormous and as the players' spokesman he invariably found himself in conflict with some people within the union as the professional revolution began to gather momentum. This led to a very uneasy relationship with the team manager, Duncan Paterson, which festered and came to a head during the 1991 World Cup. It was a difficult time for David. He felt that the players should be properly recompensed and there were various plans put in motion that would have earned the players some cash for off-field, marketing activities. They were vetoed by the SRU and, as the players' spokesman, David carried most of the flak.

In view of the quite amazing changes which the game has undergone since professionalism was endorsed by the International Board in August 1995, it can be seen that David was just three or four years ahead of his time but virtually everything which he campaigned for has come to pass. In addition, although he was castigated at the time for claiming – as we all knew – that players in other countries were being paid, within a couple of years the IB had taken its head out of the sand and had admitted that David was right and these illegal payments were, indeed, taking place on a regular, worldwide basis.

So, David it was who led us out on to Murrayfield at a slow gladiatorial pace. The atmosphere was something which I had never experienced before and nor have I since. As the game progressed, and we found ourselves under intense English pressure in the second half, we just got tighter and tighter. The team spirit and determination within that side was extraordinary. Rob Andrew played a superb game for England that day and late in the second half, with raking kicks to the corner flag, he kept us pinned down inside our own 22.

Much has been said and written about my tackle on Rory Underwood which also features in Ronnie Browne's painting commemorating the match. At the time I didn't think it was much out of the ordinary but having watched it on video tape I have to admit that it was a cracker. It was probably a good job that I got him, because if I had missed then he would have run through Gavin on

his weaker inside arc! Actually, I'm not convinced that it was a
certain try-saving tackle. There was still a bit of work for him to do
although – just in case you didn't pick it up the first time – if he had
stepped inside Gavin's right shoulder then he would have been home
and dry! I can say these things now that big brother has retired from
the international arena.

When the final whistle went the feeling was one of utter
exhilaration. I sprinted towards the tunnel, stopping on the way to
embrace an equally jubilant supporter in an enormous bear-hug. We
savoured our victory in the dressing-room and then Fin Calder said
something which I have never forgotten. He told us that we weren't
going to drink too much that night. He said that we should limit our
alcohol intake so that we could soak up every last second of the
celebrations. It was, he said, an evening that we would all want to
remember for the rest of our lives.

After the official dinner we went out to taste the atmosphere on
the streets of Edinburgh. We went to my old school-mate Remo
Maciocia's Snatcher's Bar on the Royal Mile. The place was going
crazy and it was then, when the stories began to drift back about
Grand Slam announcements being made at football grounds and
even in Jenners store on Princes Street, that it really got home to you
just what this win had meant to the people of Scotland. The feel-
good factor was immense. It wasn't just about rugby any longer. It
was something for all Scots everywhere to celebrate and an
opportunity for the nation at large to feel pretty pleased with itself.

We had heeded well Fin's warning about over-indulgence and by
the Sunday, with celebrations continuing all around us, we were still
in pretty good order. The Golf Tavern in Bruntsfield was the first
port of call on the Sabbath where Gavin and I met up with ten or
twelve of the team and then we made for Myreside where
Watsonians were staging a pretty spectacular Grand Slam brunch.

No Watsonian occasion would be complete without a special
drink to complement it and Grand Slammers – tequila and
champagne – were the order of the day. They pulled 5,000 pints at
Myreside that weekend, which gives some indication of the kind of
serious celebrating which was going on.

Most of the team were there, including the Northampton lock
Chris Gray who had decided to bring along one of his clubmates –
none other than Mr Brian Moore. To his eternal credit – and forget

for a second the pantomime villain and hate figure which Brian has become so far as a lot of Scots are concerned – he behaved with great dignity and won not a few new friends. Brian Moore, the England hooker who had less than 24 hours previously suffered the most crushing afternoon of his rugby life, got onto the Myreside stage and after some initial hissing and booing, held the audience spellbound.

He said that he was hurting still but, on the day, Scotland had wanted it more and good luck to us. He cracked a few jokes and – very significantly – wound up his impromptu speech with the firm declaration that next year England would win the Grand Slam which we had just denied them.

Brian is a very intense, intelligent and complex human being. He is also, even among his international peers who all know a thing or two about competitiveness, one of the most competitive individuals that I have ever come across. I have roomed with him with the Lions and played against him on umpteen occasions for Scotland. I think he was probably responsible, knowingly or not, for a lot of the intense rivalry which grew up around Scotland–England encounters. There were times when that rivalry got out of hand. It spilled over into the crowd and it began to get seriously unhealthy.

To try to determine who started it is a pointless exercise but there is no doubt whatsoever that, whether it be as a result of the manner in which he was portrayed in the media, or whether it was his pit-bull persona on the pitch, Scots generally did not take to Brian. And, it would seem, neither did he take to us. However, now that he has retired from international rugby it is probably true to say that one of the catalysts for what was rapidly transforming itself from intense rivalry into something approaching hatred has gone too. Certainly when we played England at Murrayfield in 1996 there didn't seem to be the same hostility which had sometimes disfigured Calcutta Cup games in recent years.

However, let's cast our minds back to the 1990 Grand Slam once again and try to place it in some kind of perspective. It was certainly one of those almost unique Scottish sporting occasions and I am immensely proud to have been part of that 1990 team, even if, as I have said earlier, I cannot escape the fact that I have been part of two other Scottish sides which had the opportunity to win Grand Slams but failed. The winning of a Grand Slam is one of my most treasured memories, but we do ourselves a disservice if we continually hark back to past glories. The Grand Slams still to come for Scotland are what should excite and inspire us now.

There is, for me, a personal postscript to the Grand Slam season. Immediately after the game my girlfriend Jenny Ovens had made her way, along with thousands of others, on to the pitch at Murrayfield. Showing great guile and determination, she even made her way into the players' tunnel and I should, of course, have popped the question there. But I didn't.

We had been at school together and going out for almost ten years. A marriage proposal was long overdue. Having failed to do so in the Murrayfield tunnel – and even amid the mayhem that was breaking out all around us, it did cross my mind a couple of times – I eventually popped the question By Royal Appointment a fortnight later, when the SRU patron, the Princess Royal hosted a private dinner for the team, wives and girlfriends at the Carlton Highland Hotel.

I approached the top table and asked the Princess Royal if I could borrow the microphone for a moment. She must have wondered what on earth was coming next but she handed me the mike and I said: 'Your Royal Highness, ladies and gentlemen, there remains one unanswered question this evening. Jenny Ovens, will you marry me?'

Jenny, I admit, was dumbstruck but with the scores of people in attendance, she wasn't really in a position to say no. It was, also, a piece of canny Hastings thinking because the SRU stumped up for all the champagne which we went on to consume that night.

Over the years, clashes between Scotland and England have inevitably been among the most hotly contested of Five Nations matches. As I've already declared, sometimes that rivalry has got out of hand but Scotland v England at anything, any sport, has that added bite to it which is missing from almost every other fixture. They are our nearest neighbours, our oldest foes and, no matter how the Five Nations' TV row turns out, our closest allies. In the words of the song, we know them so well.

There's no doubt that, close though we are (or have been) there is a different national psyche at work. A perfect example occurred after the 1995 game at Twickenham when we were both going for the Grand Slam. England won and should have been overjoyed. But they weren't. Afterwards you would have thought that they had lost. This was most apparent at the post-match banquet in London's Hilton Hotel. It was one of those rarest of rare rugby events: a mixed dinner. Wives and girlfriends were present and we decided that we would have a good night despite our defeat.

England, by comparison, were sullen and downbeat throughout. Late on, Gavin had a word in my ear and a few of us went down to Trader Vic's, the hotel cocktail bar. We ordered up a few rounds and the bar tab was standing at well over 100 quid. Gavin said he would get it and signed the bar slip 'Will Carling, Room 501'. Despite the fact that we were all there in our kilts the waitress just said: 'Thank-you, Mr Carling' and we all beat a hasty retreat! Obviously Will's fame – even that of a kilted Mr Carling – doesn't extend to the cocktail bar of the Hilton Hotel. Cheers, Will.

The England captain probably owed Gavin those drinks for what he had gone through the previous season at Murrayfield. That was the occasion when Gavin broke down in tears on live TV after Jonathan Callard had kicked a last-minute penalty goal to secure victory for England.

I had suffered a dead leg in the game and was in the medical room by the time the drama unfolded on the pitch. I heard a mighty cheer which I later learned had accompanied Gregor Townsend's drop goal that seemed to have won the game for Scotland. Minutes later there was another outburst from the crowd but this time it was the sound of 60,000 Scots groaning in unison. Ian Jardine, who had gone on as replacement for me, had been penalised for handling in a ruck in front of our posts. There was later evidence to suggest that the 'Hand of Andrew' had been the culprit and that the ref had mistaken the navy cuff of the England jersey for Jardie. In any case Jonathan Callard had kicked the goal which gave England a 15–14 victory and Scotland were devastated.

None was more devastated than Gavin who had suffered an almost identical last-minute disaster with the Lions in New Zealand the year before. How cruel sport can be. We now know that Gavin broke down in tears when Dougie Donnelly of BBC Scotland interviewed him immediately after coming off the pitch. I had, of course, seen none of this and, in fact, did not know that Gavin had broken down until I watched *Rugby Special* the following day. I was surprised but not seriously so. To come off a Test match pitch where the adrenaline is flowing and emotions are turning somersaults, straight into a TV studio is too much to ask of any player when he has just seen his hopes of victory dashed in such a cruel fashion. And remember, too, that Gavin had been the target of some severe criticism because we had not been stringing the results together. By the time I had hobbled back to the dressing-room I can tell you that if the TV cameras had been around then Gavin wouldn't have been the only player seen weeping that afternoon. There were tears aplenty from many of the Scotland team. It matters. We care. And especially so when the Auld Enemy are our opponents.

Perhaps I should devote a paragraph or three to the two Englishmen who have been my immediate opponents in so many Calcutta Cup encounters as well as being rivals and colleagues with the British Lions.

Jeremy Guscott and Will Carling have formed the English midfield, with breaks for injury, since 1989. I have played an awful lot of rugby against them. Jeremy without doubt is a player of genuine world-class. Probably he has not played as well since being forced to miss the 1994 championship season due to a long-term pelvic injury but he is still one of the classiest and sharpest individuals that I have played against. He is a silken, smooth runner whose speed off the mark is outstanding. His accuracy and timing of pass, both on a flat ball and a spin pass off both hands, is first-rate. As I've said earlier, he is also a resolute defender. He is, then, almost the complete article for a modern-day centre-three-quarter. His main weakness lies in the fact that his concentration tends to let him down. He will drift in and out of a game and if there is a criticism to be made of him at all then that must be it. That and his moodiness.

Carling's best days are, perhaps, behind him but throughout his international career he has had the England captaincy to contend with and that is a massive burden to carry. He and Guscott work very well in tandem and it was Will's poor form in 1993 which counted against him for Test selection with the Lions in New Zealand. I would have to say, though, that when he was consigned to the mid-week team he was about the only player from that side who came back from New Zealand with his reputation intact. This is another story for another chapter, but that British Lions mid-week outfit appeared to let the Test side down. Carling, though, is exonerated from that accusation which is all the more to his credit because he was obviously bitterly disappointed that the Lions captaincy had gone to Gavin and not to him.

What I find encouraging about Carling's play is that he is not frightened to attack his opposite number. Not many centres do that these days and, in recent seasons, I include myself in that category. It may well be that I have had the edge temporarily taken off my attacking prowess because of the style of rugby which Scotland had adopted under Ian McGeechan and, latterly, Dougie Morgan. It was effective and got results but it meant that, of necessity, Scottish centres were never really seen as the attacking, flair players that they could have been. There are definite signs that, with Richie Dixon and my former Watsonian team-mate David Johnston at the helm, the emphasis is changing and in 1996 I came into the championship season with a fresh attitude.

'Attack the gap' and 'space and pace' were two of the little sayings that I would constantly repeat to myself out on the pitch just to remind myself that I should never give my opposite number the easy option. Hitting too many tackle-bags and setting up yet another ruck can have a numbing effect on your attacking qualities and in 1996, in line with Scotland's determination to play the ball out of the tackle and to constantly shift the target, I endeavoured to recapture, at international level, some of the attacking flair which had been sacrificed to the cause over the years since 1986.

Nevertheless, we have played some great games and one which comes immediately to mind is the 1989 championship encounter against Ireland at Murrayfield when we won 37–21. That was a spectacular game in the true sense of the word. It was a game of technical brilliance with forwards and backs handling the ball with pace and skill. Forwards body positions were low and dynamic, while the angles of running by the backs found holes in the Irish defence.

Geech was a superbly methodical coach and I have seen few people who could read a game and analyse the opposition quite in the manner that he could. However, due almost entirely to the game-plan which Scotland stuck to throughout the earlier years of his stewardship, he never really got the best out of his backs. There were, indeed, games in which the backs clicked but it was not really until we went to New Zealand in the summer of 1990, when we produced some superb back play, that we saw the real worth of Ian's coaching.

The great thing about Geech was that he was always prepared to listen to the players. Prior to the Test matches against New Zealand we decided, as backs, that we wanted to run at the opposition. We scored five or six tries in the course of these two Tests. It was a crying shame that we didn't come away with that elusive win – especially in the second Test – but we proved that Scotland did possess backs who could run the ball with the best of them.

Lest it be thought that this is unwarranted criticism of Ian, just let me say that with the back row which he had at his disposal, allied to cracking half-backs in Gary Armstrong and Craig Chalmers, he would probably have been mad not to have had us play to our undoubted strengths. The circumstances and the personnel involved dictated how we should play, and over the years we pieced together some fantastic rugby. But this canny Yorkshire-Scot – whose astute rugby brain will be pressed into service for a record third time when the Lions go to South Africa in 1997 – was instrumental in winning only the third Grand Slam in the history of the Scottish game and for that alone we are in his debt.

6

The Lion's Pride

THE BRITISH Lions is one of those great sporting institutions which, if it didn't exist, you would have to invent. Selection for the Lions has to be the pinnacle of any Home Nation player's rugby career. There is a tradition and a mystique to the Lions which, really, transcends anything else which Northern Hemisphere rugby has to offer.

To be selected for a Lions tour, which means that you are recognised as one of the top 30 players in the British Isles and Ireland, is a singular honour, and when I was chosen alongside Gavin to go to Australia in 1989 that was special indeed – the first brothers to have been chosen to go on tour together. We were there again in 1993 when Gav captained the Lions to New Zealand. We tasted glory together in 1989 but, for me, that trip to the Land of the Long White Cloud four years later turned out to be one of the lowest of low points in my rugby career.

However, I can remember still the special feeling of pride on Saturday, 10 June 1989, when I was chosen to play in the tour opener against Western Australia. Pulling on that magnificent blood-red jersey meant that I was representing not just the British Isles but also all of those famous sporting heroes who had gone before. Sides from these islands had been touring since the turn of the century but the first official Home Unions' trip was to South Africa in 1910 and, when you consider the number of rugby legends who have worn that red shirt since, you really do appreciate the tremendous responsibility that selection for the Lions carries with it.

When you study the records of those by-gone days you wish that you could have been around when tours lasted six months and when the steamer voyage alone down to the Southern Hemisphere took a majestic and leisurely six weeks. These really were journeys of discovery to all the outposts of the Empire when among the most important pieces of kit that a player had to pack were his black tie and tails for all those grand soirées.

The first British Isles tour was to Australia in 1888. It was hit by tragedy when the captain R.L. Sedden drowned in a boating accident and when I was out in Australia someone handed me a newspaper cutting from that Victorian expedition and it concerned a game which the side had played against Northern District. It reads: 'The contest was timed to begin at a quarter past the hour of 3 o'clock but it was long after that hour before the tourists were driven on to the ground in a four-horse bus and it was after 4 o'clock when the players entered the field to the accompaniment of a hearty cheer.' It was that type of tradition and honour and, more recently, the great records of the 1971 and 1974 Lions which made you realise that you were involved in something special.

The other aspect of touring with the Lions which makes the whole thing special is that you are training, playing and living cheek-by-jowl for weeks on end with players who in a Five Nations context are fierce rivals. During a Five Nations campaign you might meet the opposition for just a couple of hours at the dinner after the game. You know everything there is to know about their rugby careers but you know next to nothing about them as individuals. When you go abroad with the Lions the special camaraderie which develops leads to lifelong friendships and that is an aspect of the game which money cannot buy.

Hardly a year seems to go by without the institution of the Lions finding itself under threat. The era of professionalism has brought with it a fresh risk to the Lions concept. The Lions are due to tour South Africa in the summer of 1997 but there must be some doubt as to whether the tour will go ahead even if the issue of England's participation within the Five Nations is resolved. Players will be under contract to their clubs and to the international unions with all the difficulties that this imposes. Additionally, unlike individual unions which can benefit from the revenue raised by incoming tours, the Lions is a unique institution which does not have this regular source of income. In those circumstances, the problem of just who is going to pay the players when they are in South Africa is one which, at the time of writing, is exercising the minds of those who feel, as I do, that we have in the Lions something far too special to be allowed to disappear.

The fact, too, that the playing calendar in the Northern Hemisphere becomes more and more crowded with every year that passes means that there might not be time to fit in Lions tours every four years. As the game continues to develop, with the European Cup promising to take off in a big way, the World Cup and World Cup Sevens established as permanent fixtures in the calendar and the possibility of the Five Nations Championship developing into a proper European Championship along the lines of the football model, then the Lions begin to look more and more like an endangered species.

As I've indicated, I'm a great supporter of the Lions and would be sorry to see the concept fall by the wayside, but in the years ahead there is no doubt in my mind that if it is to survive then its corner is going to have to be fought very fiercely indeed.

During a Lions tour year the Five Nations games become a series of trials for the trip. Back in 1989 Scotland had played some very attractive rugby and there was a very real chance that we would supply a fair contingent to the Australian tour party.

In the event nine Scots made the trip: Gavin, Peter Dods, Gary Armstrong, Craig Chalmers, Fin Calder, John Jeffrey, David Sole, Derek White and me. With Fin as captain and Ian McGeechan as coach the tour had a real tartan look to it. The choice of Finlay as captain was inspired. He is a really charismatic character and as the tour progressed the strength of his personality shone through. From the very first day he brought all the players together and told us that he would not stand for the development of nationalistic cliques. That is always a danger with the Lions and unless it is nipped in the bud early on it is something which threatens the cohesiveness of the squad. There were occasions, at dinner for example, when there would be an English table, an Irish table and so on. However, once a few fines had been levied that was soon stopped and the tour party developed into a very happy band of brothers with individual nationalities forgotten in the interests of the common cause.

That was one of the happiest tours that I have been on. Clive Rowlands was a superb manager. He steered the entire party in the right direction. He invariably struck the right note and, at the many functions and receptions which are the touring players' lot, the direction in which he steered us was resolutely to the exit before the swarms of well-meaning but too often boring alickadoos could get their hooks into us.

Clive really came into his own after the first Test when we suffered our first defeat of the tour and had experienced the humiliation of being outplayed in virtually every department. Clive knew that the time for smooth-talking was over and, basically, he blew a gasket and told us that we were playing for the pride of the Lions and that, from that point onwards, the badge that we wore on our jerseys would just keep on getting bigger and bigger.

My rivals for a Test berth on that trip were Mike Hall, Brendan Mullin, Jeremy Guscott and John Devereux so the competition was always going to be fierce, but what was important was that we Scots had got ourselves tremendously fit before leaving for Australia. We had been on special training programmes overseen by Derrick Grant in the Borders and Dougie Morgan at Murrayfield, and by the time we got on that plane at Heathrow the Scots were certainly heading the field in the fitness stakes.

One of the most significant results of professionalism is going to be that players will have the time to become fitter than they have ever been before. However, under the old – if we can call it that – era it was while on tour that players played and trained as professionals in all but name. Especially on an eight-week Lions tour when you would be training every day and playing twice a week, most players achieved levels of fitness that they could only dream about during a Five Nations season.

When you are touring, and once the party has settled down into a Saturday team and a mid-week team, the main focus tends to be on the Saturday, or Test, side but anybody who has been abroad on tour knows that it is absolutely essential that the mid-week side performs well and keeps on bringing home the bacon. With the Lions in 1989, and ultimately under the leadership of Donal Lenihan, the success of the mid-week side – 'Donal's Doughnuts' they were christened – was crucial to the success of the tour as a whole.

The tour opener was against Western Australia in Perth. I'm a great believer in the truth of the old adage that the performance in the first game sets the tone and the standard for the rest of the trip and because Australia B were next up it was particularly important that we threw down the gauntlet in no uncertain fashion at the Perry Lakes Stadium which had been the venue for the 1962 Commonwealth Games.

The game was played on a super surface and in fantastic weather with the temperature sitting at 19 degrees centigrade. Just twenty minutes into the game the Irish fly-half Paul Dean went off injured and that was his tour over. It's always a sad sight to see a player leaving the field injured and especially so when it's an injury which means that he is going to be on the next plane home – a heartbreaking fate which was awaiting me four years later in New Zealand.

Craig Chalmers came off the bench and played extremely well. He had first been capped that year and was now in pole position for the Lions stand-off berth – a remarkable rise to the top by any standards. We won the game 44–0. Brendan Mullin had a hat-trick and I had a try as well, so the tour had got off to a very encouraging start.

I have almost always kept a personal diary wherever I am on rugby business throughout the world. My tour log completed after that opening game declares: 'It was a great honour to pull on the Lions jersey with all the tradition and the great players behind it. Just before kick-off my mind clicked back to the photographs I had seen of the red jersey being worn on previous tours and in particular the book of the '71 tour, *The Roaring Lions*. Adrenalin flowed and off we went. It has been almost two months since my last fifteen-a-side game. That showed throughout the team during the opening exchanges. It was a tough first period with us not taking all our chances and Paul Dean coming off with an injured knee after 25 minutes. It was 8–0 at half-time and we knew that we had to raise the tempo. The forwards began to win quicker ball and the game began to flow. We had some great moves. Brendan Mullin scored a hat-trick and I took a lot of pleasure from running in one myself. Peter Dods had a nightmare with his kicking but he eventually came good and we won 44–0.'

We were well pleased with our opening performance. The week in Perth was absolutely superb. We were well looked after throughout. One of the marketing ploys which the local union employed to publicise the match was for a couple of the Lions to visit rugby clubs in the area. Bob Norster and I were deputed to go down to the

Associates' Rugby Club on the Thursday before the game where we were eye-witnesses to a novel ploy designed to get the guys along to training. They put a topless barmaid behind the bar but you weren't allowed in unless you had actually been training. That kind of thing might even catch on at Myreside!

Next stop was Melbourne which provided the opportunity to catch up again with brother Graeme. Melbourne is a hotbed of that crazy game Aussie Rules football and rugby union barely gets a look in. But we were due to meet a very strong Australia B side and that gave an opportunity for all of those who hadn't played in the tour opener to stretch their legs.

I sat on the bench for the game which was played in Olympic Park, the venue for the 1956 Olympics. The game was played at night in extremely damp conditions – typical Melbourne weather according to Graeme – and the guys came away with a 23–18 win.

The trusty old tour diary recounts: 'What a battle that was with Australia taking a 14–7 lead. By that time the pitch was cutting up badly and there was an annoying light drizzle. The boys fought hard and came good after a bout of pressure saw them pull away to 23–14. Gavin had come on to a good game and two good penalty kicks by him followed by two tries, one of which he converted. However, Australia came back to score another pushover try to give the boys an anxious last five minutes. We weathered the storm and the Big W had been achieved – a confidence boosting win.'

There had been criticism before the tour got under way about the in-depth strength of Australian rugby and questions asked about whether they were strong enough to host a full-blooded Lions tour. We always believed that they were and that second game against the Australian B side – which admittedly contained quite a few capped players – proved that we were going to be forced to work hard for victory outside the Test matches.

The constantly moving feast that is a rugby tour next moved on to Brisbane where Queensland – traditionally one of the strongest Oz states – were lying in wait. They had always been one of the most powerful outfits in the Southern Hemisphere and, that season in particular, they had gone 25 games without a loss. They had beaten the All Blacks and the Lions in the past and, by this time in the tour, we knew that our selection would be getting close to that which would play in the first Test.

I was chuffed to be picked and my centre partner for this big, big game was the Welshman John Devereux. I had partnered Brendan Mullin in the opening game, while John and Jeremy had been the centres against Australia B. Obviously the management were looking at the various permutations with the first Test still four games away.

England's Rob Andrew had just joined the tour as the replacement for Paul Dean. He had missed out on selection and with Dean's departure Craig Chalmers was the nominal first-choice fly-half. On tour, though, fortunes can change more rapidly than the weather and, as we now know, Rob made a late run down the stand rail to snatch first pick status from Craig.

This was a helluva game. It was an incredibly physical encounter. Mike Hall, who was playing on the wing, was caught at the bottom of a ruck where he received a hefty blow to the head and had to go off. The Lions pack played a stormer and really met fire with fire. We were down at half-time but went on to win 19–15. The other statistic which came to the fore was 24–0 in our favour. That was the stitch count.

The Queenslanders had set out their stall with a big, physical pack which was intended to rough us up in the forward exchanges. It didn't work out that way and, really, this was the game in which all the Australian media hype about Lions thugs made its first appearance. The Mike Hall injury had led to a punch-up and it was becoming clear that there was little love lost between the Aussies and the Lions. We didn't want to become known as a dirty team but we were determined that we weren't going to be intimidated by the Australians and there is no doubt, whatsoever, that this was their intention.

Out and out thuggery – despite what the Australian media said at the time – was never part of our game-plan but we had decided that if a Lions player was singled out for attention by the opposition then the rest of the side would come to his aid, pronto. Rugby is a hard, physical contact sport and one thing which you can never allow the opposition to do is to intimidate you. We were determined to meet fire with fire.

We had been in the country for over two weeks by this time and it had been an incredibly intensive period. Touring is like that. Ideally, by this time the squad is really gelling and there are times when you feel like a commando squad operating behind enemy

lines. We felt, though, that we could relax just a little on our trip
north to the holiday haven of Cairns where we were to take on
Queensland B. We had already beaten the best that Queensland
could throw at us and the prospect of playing their second-string side
in Cairns felt almost as if we were on our holidays.

I had been selected for bench duty but had pulled up short with a
hamstring tug a couple of days before the game and on the morning
of the match I decided to pull out.

I was disappointed, the more so because the weather was
absolutely superb and it was a bit of a downer in such glorious
conditions to be not quite as fit as you would like to be. At the back
of my mind, too, was the fact that the first Test was just a week and
a half away and this was not the time to be getting injured, no matter
how mild the injury was.

Queensland B were disposed of 30–6. Even with a 6.45 p.m.
kick-off the temperature was still sitting at 25 degrees and with
Cairns being the back-packing capital of Australia the crowd was
made up of young folk from all over the world. This was Rob
Andrew's first game on tour and he played exceptionally well.
Suddenly, a lot of the guys had seen a side of Rob's game which we
hadn't witnessed before. He was running the ball, making a lot of
telling breaks and, all in all, put in a really commanding
performance. He was putting down a very firm marker indeed for
Test selection. Ian McGeechan's coaching influence was beginning
to tell on the backs. The continuity which he demanded from his
Scotland side was starting to rub off on the Lions – the angles of
running, the weight of pass and all the drills which we had benefited
from in Scotland were making their mark across the entire side and
we reckoned that we were beginning to look like a particularly
handy pride of Lions.

Cairns was a wonderful destination. We swam off the Great
Barrier Reef, played a lot of golf and spent one afternoon river-
rafting. It's not always blood, sweat and tears on rugby tours. The
best tours are the ones where a satisfactory compromise is reached
between the hard graft of training and playing and recreational
distractions. Blood, sweat and (a few) beers makes for the happiest
rugby trips abroad.

The faithful tour diary records how much I enjoyed the Cairns'
experience. 'We moved into the Cairns Hilton – yet another

internationally acclaimed hostelry. We really are up in the tropics here and the humidity is something else.'

Next up were New South Wales in Sydney and, as we flew south, we knew that our brief holiday was over. NSW were one of Australia's top state sides, laced throughout with internationalists. I wasn't selected for the game and began to suffer a bout of the jitters. The first Test was now just a week away and I feared that I might have blown my chances of selection because of the hamstring situation in Cairns. Jeremy Guscott and John Devereux were preferred at centre and, although I was back on the bench, I was by no means certain that this was a good omen for the Test. Additionally, I had niggling doubts about the hamstring and that is not the best frame of mind in which to approach any game, let alone a Test match in seven days' time.

It was, though, a cracker of a game, played in the magnificent North Sydney Oval stadium. The Lions were down 9–7 at half-time but then we stretched ahead to 20–12 with 12 minutes to go. My diary records: 'A good try was conjured up by NSW and converted from the touchline. Just after that, John Devereux went down injured. He was stretchered off with a bad ankle and I came on. It was a desperate situation. I had been trying to warm up during the game and the hamstring was niggling. I had just been on the pitch for a minute when I felt another tug. I thought it had gone but I stayed on the pitch and, with two minutes to go the score was 21–20 to NSW. Craig Chalmers dropped his third goal in the dying seconds to give us a close-run win and our unbeaten record was kept intact.'

We next played New South Wales B at Dubbo. This was a difficult time for the Lions in terms of injuries. I wasn't happy with my hamstring and had tried to get out of being selected for the NSW B game just days before the opening Test match.

However, I was told that I would have to prove my fitness by playing and the tour diary records: 'This is it. It is make or break. I've to play against NSW B and the hamstring is either going to go and it's all over, or I can stake a claim for Test selection. Chris Oti seemed doubtful when he was looked at by the doc and it will be decided later whether he is to be sent home with cartilage trouble. Rob Andrew, Peter Dods and myself all have hamstring problems. John Devereux has an ankle twist. Ieuan Evans has a problem with a calf muscle. Donal Lenihan has a bad shoulder and Mike Teague isn't right either. I'm not too confident but it appears the problem with my leg is not on the hamstring, itself but old scar tissue. Because I felt it tug on Saturday I don't give it too much hope. It's ruining me at the moment going through so many emotions. I've just got to relax and give it my best shot.'

This was Test match week and nerves were jangling. Nobody had ever said as much but I knew that if I didn't prove myself against New South Wales B then I was probably going to be sent home. The problem seemed to be related to the hamstring injury which had ended my 1987 World Cup. I had tweaked the hamstring in training before going out to Australia with the Lions but had kept quiet about it. It was just this single strand of muscle, and old scar tissue, which was threatening my Lions tour. In these circumstances you keep your blackest thoughts to yourself but it wasn't a happy period for me. I had a brief chat with Kevin Murphy, the physio, and he strapped the leg up so securely and severely that I could hardly run. I record in the diary: 'After a good night's sleep in the circumstances I concentrated on getting myself mentally fit for the game. Because of the facilities, or lack of them, at the ground, we had to change in the hotel. I was strapped up by Kevin so that made a difference and really boosted my confidence. The strapping seemed to make all the difference.'

Ten minutes into the game I got the ball with about 30 metres to run for the line and, from a photograph that was taken at the time, you can just see the look of desperate concentration on my face. It looked as though I was focused resolutely on making the line but, in reality, what I was doing was concentrating like never before on not over-stretching the hamstring.

It turned out to be quite a tough game. We got off to a poor start but rattled off three good tries in the second half and came away with a solid 39–19 win. More importantly from a personal point of view, I had come through the game unscathed and my chances of Test selection remained intact. But I was kidding myself. Deep down, I knew fine well that I couldn't be selected. I had played against NSW B while not being fully fit and when the Test side was selected the following day I knew beforehand that my chances of making it were slim.

I wrote at the time: 'The team was announced prior to training and, unfortunately, I've not made it. I'm disappointed but having informed Fin Calder last night that I had played to only 80 per cent of my capacity against New South Wales B, that counted against me and Mike Hall will play alongside Brendan Mullin in the centre. It would have been easy to have said that I was alright but I know in my own mind that I took the correct decision. I want to play for the Lions in a Test but I want to do so when I am 100 per cent fit so that I can play to the best of my ability. I'll get another chance on Tuesday against ACT and hopefully I'll be able to stake my claim for a place in the second Test. That's a realistic aim to have and I'm going for it.'

Up until that point in the tour there had been no real indication as to what the Test line-up was going to be. It was, perhaps, a reflection of the strength in depth of that tour party that so many Test places were still up for grabs. Would Craig Chalmers, who was now seen as first-choice fly-half, hold off the challenge of the recently arrived Rob Andrew? The selectors were spoiled for choice in the back row. Calder, Derek White, Dean Richards, John Jeffrey, Andy Robinson, Mike Teague – every one of them in his way a marvellous player. What about the scrum-half position – Rob Jones or Gary Armstrong? The management faced these kinds of choices right through the squad. It was a glorious position for the selectors to be in but it made it a pretty tense and tough tour for the players.

So, the side which was selected to fly the Lions banner in front of a capacity 40,000 crowd at the Sydney Football Stadium was: Gavin Hastings, Ieuan Evans, Mike Hall, Brendan Mullin, Rory Underwood, Craig Chalmers, Rob Jones, David Sole, Brian Moore, Dai Young, Paul Ackford, Robert Norster, Derek White, Dean Richards and Finlay Calder.

We had won all of our games thus far and we were very confident indeed going into that first Test. Too confident. This was what we had all been waiting for. The mid-week stuff was now out of the way. This was Test match rugby. It was what we had come all that way for.

I had trained on the morning of the game at the Test match venue. It turned out to be one of my best training sessions of the tour. I was sprinting flat out without any sign of the hamstring niggle which had meant I wasn't considered for the Test side. Four days earlier I had written in the tour diary that I wanted to play Test match rugby only when I was fit. Yet there I was on the morning of the match feeling as sharp as a tack. These four days had made all the difference in the world. But that's touring. Everything has to work absolutely in your favour on the chosen day or you are sidelined. I was obviously disappointed to have been ruled out of consideration for the Test but I took consolation from the fact that I now knew beyond doubt that I would be fit for the Tuesday game against ACT and that was where I would put my hand up for the second Test.

I watched the first Test from the stand and what a humiliating experience it turned out to be. Basically, Australia had done their homework and they came out with all guns firing. Steve Cutler and Bill Campbell dominated the lineout and we made too many errors behind the scrum. Although Mike Hall had been chosen originally as a winger, because of the injury situation he was pressed into service in the centre. The combination of Mike and Brendan didn't seem to click. Australia got off to a flying start when Scott Gourlay scored between the posts. Thereafter the Lions were playing catch-up rugby.

My diary declares: 'At half-time it was 15–6 against us and it was obvious that lineout ball was proving very difficult to win. The scrum was very solid but the backs were too eager to spread the ball wide without first committing the Aussie defence. Although difficult to watch, and although I am loath to criticise, you could see from the stand the way in which we should have used our possession. Gavin missed a few kicks at goal and Australia picked up their game. In the second half everything was going Australia's way. Their kicks were landing just inches from touch and bouncing out. We were well stuffed and the final score of 30–12 in Australia's favour dealt a real blow to us. Our pride and confidence has been hurt.'

I went down to the changing-room immediately afterwards and it was an incredible experience. I don't think that any of us had appreciated that Australia were capable of playing such dominant rugby. The atmosphere in the stadium had been fantastic and that had acted as a real spur to the Wallabies. We shouldn't take anything away from the Australian performance that day. They played superbly well and Michael Lynagh had one of those days when every kick was inch perfect. Every move seemed to come off and that, coupled with a dominant performance by their pack, meant that we weren't at the races.

Frankly, we were distraught. We had been wiped off the face of the earth and there were still four weeks of the tour to go. The only way was up. Fin Calder said afterwards to the Press that his Lions would never play so badly again while Mike Griffiths said, privately, that the Lion had a thorn in its paw. That was when Clive Rowlands the manager told us that from then on the Lions badge would just keep on getting bigger and bigger.

The primary concern of the media after that first Test was to find a scapegoat and Fin Calder was it. There was widespread speculation in the papers as to whether Fin should actually drop himself as another Scottish Lions captain, Mike Campbell-Lamerton, had done in 1966. Fin actually wrote a letter to his wife in which he speculated on the pros and cons of making himself unavailable for selection for the second Test. The pressures were enormous. While the UK papers were firing the bullets at us, the Australian Press were firing off in another direction. Early on they had been foaming at the mouth over the physicality of our forward play. After the Wallabies' victory in the first Test, the Australian newspapers reported: 'Swift boot to the aura of British Isles "Thugby" stars'. That's called having your cake and eating it. We had gone from being hairy-arsed monsters to a bunch of soft-centred Poms. Hang around boys. The show ain't over yet.

We flew down to Canberra the day after the Test to make ourselves ready for the game against Australian Capital Territories. This was crunch time. It was make or break. We had to get the tour back on the rails with a convincing victory over ACT and, from a personal point of view, this was my chance to force my way back into Test reckoning. Our future depended upon Donal and his Doughnuts. Donal Lenihan had been leading the mid-week side with great Irish panache. He was one of the great tour humorists and it was his kind of good humour which can really come to the rescue of a tour when it seems that everything is going wrong.

My tour diary records: 'We have had the usual round of team meetings at which the theme is geared to winning and playing well. The pressure and focus of the whole squad is on us. There is a tremendous atmosphere in the lead-up to the game. There is a good feeling. Donal gave us an inspired team-talk before we left the hotel for the ground. He left us knowing in no uncertain terms just what was expected from each and every one of us. However, after 25 minutes we must have wondered where it was all going wrong. We were 21–8 down and getting a real roasting. What made matters worse was that every time ACT scored the public address system played this annoying Kookaburras' song. It went something like this:

"Kookaburras come from the ACT. We're invincible when we play rugbee. Canberra Kookaburras etc, etc, etc." Absolutely dreadful and really, really annoying. Our two tries, by Wade Dooley through the lineout, and Mike Hall running off a dummy bullet which is an intrusion by the full-back between the centres followed by a standard mis-move, were both crackers. Our transgressions and lack of control cost us dearly and we had a disappointing first half.'

So there we were having just lost the Test match and now we were 40 minutes into the game which was going to be the tour saviour and we were 21–11 down at the turn. Not good.

The diary takes up the story: 'However, with the wind and sun at our backs, as well as playing downhill (!) the conditions were in our favour. We scrambled back with a penalty try and a cracker of a score by Gary Armstrong who broke from a scrum 20 yards out and showed his real class as he burst through for the try. Peter Dods had his kicking boots on and we took all the penalties given to us which stretched our lead. Personally, my leg felt great and although I had a quiet game I got an interception try from 10 yards out for my third try of the tour. The final score of 41–25 represented a rousing comeback and when we walked into the changing-room the rest of the party were there applauding us in. It meant a lot to everyone. We had won and that victory had lifted the whole tour party. This has set us on our way towards the second Test.'

I reckoned that I was in the frame for Test selection. I had been playing alongside Jeremy Guscott and, from my point of view, the combination had been working well. The side was initially to be announced the following day and the diary relates: 'This was always going to be a long day. With all the travelling it has been decided not to announce the side for the Test until our arrival in Brisbane. An early start, at 7 a.m., tested our wake-up capabilities. We flew from Canberra to Sydney and from Sydney on to Brisbane. By the time we arrived we were running out of light but we managed to get along to the Test venue at Ballymore and it was almost dark by the time the training session had ended. The side will now be announced tomorrow.'

The tour log entry for that anxious day of reckoning declares: 'The team has been announced and I am delighted to be in. Not only because I wanted it so much but because with Gavin playing and our parents out in support it is a great honour for the whole family. That's especially true for our mum and dad who have been our greatest supporters from school matches on Saturday mornings right through Watsonians and Edinburgh, age-group and schoolboy internationals, Scotland and the World Cup. Finally we are both playing for the Lions. It is fantastic. You couldn't wish for better parents. It's especially good that we're both playing on Saturday because mum and dad have to go back to Edinburgh after the Test match. Rob Andrew, Jeremy Guscott, Wade Dooley and Mike Teague are the other changes in the team. We now have the responsibility of carrying the Lions hopes on our shoulders. But not only that. We have the chance to win.'

We knew the task that we faced. It was simple. We had to win. If we lost then the series was a goner and we were in the situation of having to spend three weeks in the country having lost the Test series. That is a mighty spur. Australia had been more street-wise in the opening Test. We knew that we had to match them in that department. We were going to grind them down up front and from that we hoped for decent ball with which to attack them in the backs. But the key lay with the forwards. The Lions pack had taken a mauling in the first Test and that was the area that we had to sort out first and foremost.

We prepared for that second Test like a team of crack commandos going into battle. I, though, had some personal preparation to take care of. Before leaving the UK I had accepted a bet from a friend, Steven Gilhooley, who had packed in his job and travelled out to support the Lions. The bet was that if I got selected for a Test berth then I would have to get a crazy haircut. When the Test side was announced Steven turned up at the team hotel and dragged me off to a hairdressing salon. That was when the speed-lines made their appearance. It's strange the things that stick in your mind, but the young lady who razored the stripes into the side of my scalp was called Leith. She was so nervous about shaving the lines, and her hands were so jittery, that I ended up not with the delicate pin-stripes which had been the plan, but two half-inch wide gashes above the ears. It must have looked stupid and, truthfully, it was a horrendous haircut but it was a statement of intent. I used to get very wound up in these days before big games and the stripes were a physical reminder to me that I had to be utterly focused on what was going to be the biggest game of my rugby life. Daft, I know, but if it works then don't knock it.

The countdown was now on with a vengeance. We were very apprehensive as we left the hotel for the ground. We knew that we were under the most intense of pressures. We just had to win.

I recorded at the time: 'By the time we reached Ballymore we were more than ready. It was a brilliant feeling to run out on to the pitch and represent the British Lions in a Test match. What a fiery start. Robert Jones hit Nick Farr-Jones at the side of a scrum. I don't know why he did it but Rob stamped his studs right on Nick Farr-Jones's toe. Farr-Jones punched Rob, the forwards looked up and all hell broke loose. It was like a '99' had been called. That was the most fiery start that I have ever seen to an international. There was no way that we were going to lose on this occasion.

'There were a few other incidents throughout the game but our pack was leading the way. They produced some good second-phase ball that might have been better used, with me kicking away one ball in particular which I should have run. However, the game was always going to be won up front where Mike Teague and Dean Richards were leading the charge. At half-time we were 9–6 down but there was still a tremendous feeling within the team that we would win. As the game wore on the backs started coming more and more into the game. With a great break-out from our own 22 Jeremy Guscott handed on to me before I got caught on Australia's 22. Rory Underwood almost scored and then Michael Lynagh missed a crucial penalty which came off the upright. After another good break-out we set up good second-phase ball before I gave a long, tired, looping pass to Gavin who picked up the bouncing ball to score in the corner. Suddenly, with five minutes to go, we found ourselves in the lead. It was an incredible feeling. Could we hold on to square the series and save the tour?

'Two box balls which were spilled by David Campese led to Jeremy Guscott scoring a great individual try beside the posts when he chipped through and collected. It had been a great performance and the scenes in the dressing-room were wild. We were all overjoyed and, not holding back my emotions, I shed a few tears. I felt I could have played better and made more of the ball that I got but I've now got my confidence back and I know I can do better. I was overjoyed to see my folks before we went to the reception. I'm going out to celebrate the night away.'

The Battle of Ballymore, as the game was soon known, had been

The Queen and I. HM visited George Watson's College in 1982. I'm the apprehensive one standing third from the right.

Captain of Scottish Schools. The side which played England at Vale of Lune, Lancaster, in 1982.

Great hair! Michael Lynagh lies prostrate at my feet and one of his Aussie Schoolboy team-mates tries unsuccessfully to wrestle me to the ground. We were hammered. Murrayfield, 1982.

Freedom. Celebrating our final day at school, with chums Colin Hunter and Alan Beattie.

It's a tough life. Hong Kong Sevens, 1986, and fellow Co-optimists Eric Paxton, Andrew Ker and Bob Hogarth soak up the oriental sun.

It's all yours brother. Gavin and I make our Scotland debuts against France in 1986. (Allsport)

Celtic cousins. Scotland's Five Nations' clashes have, invariably, produced some fantastic matches. Here I seem to have got the better of my old sparring partner Brendan Mullin. (James Galloway, *The Herald*)

Eye on the ball. A training session before the game against Wales in 1989. Ian McGeechan watches my every move. (Allsport)

Ya beauty. Celebrating Jeremy Guscott's winning try for the British Lions in the crucial second Test at Ballymore, Brisbane, in 1989. Note the 'speed stripes' in the hair which were the result of a wager. (Allsport)

Hanging on in there. With the British Lions in Australia in 1989. Ian Williams isn't going anywhere. (Allsport)

Touchdown. A try for me against Australian Capital Territories with the British Lions in 1989. (Bob Thomas Sports Photography)

Banzai. In full flight against Japan during our RWC 1991 encounter at Murrayfield. (David Gibson, Fotosport)

Leading the Barbarians against New Zealand at the Arms Park in 1993 was one of the highlights of my career. (David Gibson, Fotosport)

The chase is on: Didier Camberabero and I are in full flight at the Parc des Princes in 1993. I won the race. France won the match. (David Gibson, Fotosport)

Spin it wide: Parc des Princes, 1993. (David Gibson, Fotosport)

such a nip-and-tuck encounter that we were all drained afterwards. Beforehand, Ian McGeechan had decided that we should put Campese under a few high balls. Robert Jones had been working all week at putting Campo under pressure. His hard work, and McGeechan's foresight, paid off because it was from a kick for Campese that Jeremy Guscott scored his try.

Gavin's try, which I had played a part in, was also crucial. When I threw out the pass I was absolutely knackered. There had been a lot of end-to-end stuff and it had taken its toll. Gavin picked the ball up on the bounce and then handed off the Wallaby centre Dominic McGuire. Gav has a photograph of him getting to his feet just after scoring and, if you look closely, you can see that his eyes are glazed.

The fact of the matter is that he was concussed. When I threw out the looping pass Gavin saw three balls in front of him. Luckily, he chose to pick up the one in the middle. If he had gone for either of the others then there would have been no try and the history of the 1989 Lions tour to Australia would not have turned out as it did! The Test was won 19–12 and the show was back on the road with a vengeance.

The Australian media went into overdrive after that game. Once again we were the Lions thugs. We had never made physical intimidation part of our game-plan but we were equally sure that if it came to a rough-house we weren't going to come out losers. We had already lost Mike Hall to Aussie thuggery and he was going to be the last. In a touring situation, on the other side of the world, you are 15 guys against the whole of Australia. These things have to be done.

There was no mid-week game between the second and third Tests so those who had missed out on selection in Brisbane had no real opportunity to advance their causes for the Sydney rematch. Before moving to Sydney we spent a couple of days at Surfers' Paradise on the Gold Coast where we recharged the batteries in preparation for the Test decider.

As expected, there were no changes to the side and, while the Aussie media and the Australian RFU continued their rantings about the so-called Battle of Ballymore, we got on quietly with our planning for the Test.

To the great surprise of many and, no doubt, the disappointment of the Australian media, the game was played in a fine spirit throughout. We won the game and clinched the series with a 19–18 victory.

My tour diary records the day thus: 'I'll look back at this match, no doubt, in a few years and reflect that it was one of the most intense and exciting that I have ever played in. The setting of the Sydney Football Stadium lends itself to a fantastic atmosphere. Before the game we had psyched ourselves up to a state of controlled aggression. As the national anthems were sung the atmosphere was electric. Robert Jones and Nick Farr-Jones had another minor altercation by the side of the pitch but nothing like on the same scale as Ballymore. The referee Rene Hourquet nipped it in the bud and it was clear that neither side really wanted a repeat of what had happened the previous week.

'It was a fast game with both sides seeking territorial control by means of long touch-finders. Some didn't quite make it, resulting in a few counter-attacks. Gavin had his kicking boots on and the Lions took the lead 9–3 with three penalties from him. The forwards were doing well and I felt that the backs used the ball sensibly throughout. Just on half-time Brian Moore took a crucial strike against the head on our line but from the lineout we fumbled the ball to give Australia another attacking scrum. Lynagh, threw two dummy passes, pulled Jeremy Guscott out of position and fed Ian Williams who went in for a try. Lynagh converted and, after just one mistake, we had let them back into the game.

'It was 9–9 at half-time and both sides had everything to play for. Just after the restart Lynagh kicked a penalty but then a blunder by Campese, when he threw an in-goal pass to Greg Martin, let Ieuan Evans in for a score. That was a huge psychological blow to the Australians. Two penalty goals by Gavin stretched our lead as the game entered the most exciting period of Test match rugby that I have ever played in. I never felt that Australia would win but they pulled back two penalty goals by Mike Lynagh. We were seven long minutes from victory. Australia threw everything at us but our determination was fantastic. Even after a desperate counter-attack from Australia's dead-ball line in the final seconds, the game was not won until we had killed the ball. The whistle went and victory was ours.

'We did a lap of honour to thank the British support in the stadium and, back in the changing-room, the scenes of jubilation were of an order that I had not experienced before. These were touching and emotional moments. I was thrilled for the fact that we had done it for everybody in the squad, for our supporters, and most of all for Jenny and our folks.'

That was how it felt at the time. It feels much the same now. It still ranks, even with the passing of the years, as one of the great moments of my rugby life and as one of the great moments in the long and honourable history of the British Lions. After the final whistle, I had stuffed the match ball up my jumper and, I fear, vanity got the better of me. There were TV cameras and Press photographers all over the place and, with the ball inside my shirt, I looked nine months pregnant. That looks pretty stupid, I thought, so I ran across to Gavin and handed him the ball. 'You'll probably want this,' I said to him. The upshot is that he now has the ball used in one of the most important games in the history of British rugby. It's been beautifully signed by both teams and whenever I see it I kick myself for handing it over. That's one that I may have to claim back in the years to come.

Looking back, I believe that we would still have won even if it had not been for David Campese's incredibly lackadaisical pass to Greg Martin. Rob Andrew had unsuccessfully had a shot at a drop-goal and there was Campese deciding, half-heartedly, to take it out and he gave a looping pass to Martin. To his credit, Ieuan had followed up the kick and he was right on the spot when Campese's pass hit the deck. The ridicule which Campese received from his own media was absolutely staggering. I felt sorry for him then but he had the last laugh two years later when he, more or less, won the World Cup for Australia because of his magnificent form. You have to look at all the great players and realise that, at some time or another, they will make mistakes. There's no doubt that Campese is one of the all-time greats of the game. Despite the fact that he has been in and out of favour with the Australian selectors and that he must be in the twilight of his career you would find it hard to get odds against him getting his cherished 100 caps for the Wallabies.

My diary entry for the day after that historic victory reads: 'Having eventually made it to bed around 5 a.m. I still managed to get up early for breakfast and was joined by Brian Moore and Wade Dooley. Still half-cut, we swapped stories about the previous night. Brian was apparently found walking over the Sydney Harbour

Bridge – literally from one side to the other – before being rescued by *The Times*'s rugby writer David Hands who gave him a lift in his car back to the hotel! Brother Graeme joined us for coffee along with friends Robin and Kevin Murray and Graeme's wife Jacqui.

'After lunch we headed from the North Sydney Travelodge to the Newcastle International Beach Hotel, a real dive of a place on the Newcastle beach front. The bus trip was uneventful although there were a few beers consumed along the way.

'That evening we headed off to one of the local rugby clubs who put on a smashing spit-roast of lamb. We were still celebrating our win and it was a great way to relax on the Sunday after that magnificent victory. As Mike Teague, Rob Jones, Craig Chalmers, Rob Andrew and I were still 'thirsty' we headed out for a few beers to a bar called The Brewery. Having been noticed we were invited by the manager to stay on for a few more. We moved on to another pub where we tucked in to champagne and cocktails. It ended up being one of the best nights of the tour. The best sessions are always informal, impromptu occasions. The mood was just right and we all had a wonderful time.'

So that was the series won and we were off to Newcastle for two days of partying and a game against the New South Wales Country XV. We visited the Wyndham Estate, created when George Wyndham left the UK for Australia in 1888, and which boasts Australia's oldest vineyard. They hosted a wonderful lunch and, with everybody still celebrating Saturday's victory, it was one of those occasions that will live long in the memory. Ieuan Evans fell for the spoon on the head scam whereby two players are blindfolded and, each with a spoon in his mouth, they have to tap the other on the top of the skull with the spoon. However, unknown to one of the protagonists, the tapping is actually being done by a third person. It loses something in the telling but poor Ieuan, blindfolded as he was, just couldn't work out how Fin Calder was managing to make so many hits with his spoon. It was one of those fun touring days when you could relax, switch off and savour the moment.

The NSW Country XV were dispatched 72–3 and the game was notable mostly for a new move, code named 'Gallipoli', which the Aussies tried to pull off. It was novel. It was daring. It was dangerous but it was also absolutely bloody hilarious. At scrum-time their blind-side winger jumped on to the back of his No. 8 and ran over the top of the scrummage, only to stumble and fall at the feet of Derek White and Gary Armstrong who inflicted salutary and condign punishment.

The tour was hurtling to a close and all that remained was the final game against a combined Australia–New Zealand ANZACS XV. My tour log recounts the lead-up to the game: 'We trained at Brisbane Boys' College. Had a fantastic session. We returned later in the afternoon for a game of cricket. This was an absolute classic. We are by now a very close-knit group of players and we really enjoy each other's company. Fin Calder's side scored 102 runs. Thirteen wickets fell at an even pace. The weather was beautiful as Donal's Doughnuts padded up to bat and chase the Calder side's total. By the time I came in to bat we were well on our way to victory. Steve Smith, who had given away 25 off his previous over, came back to bowl and with six runs to get and three wickets remaining, I went for the big hit. I was out and Stevie went on to take his hat-trick, capturing the wickets of John Jeffrey and Peter Dods. The Irish hooker takes a hat-trick on tour. It was an unbelievable finish to what was felt by everyone to be one of the best days of the trip.'

So, only the tour finale against the ANZACS was left. The Bledisloe Cup between Australia and New Zealand was imminent and, to our disappointment, quite a number of the All Blacks pulled out. They didn't want to be associating with their soon-to-be deadly rivals with their equivalent of our Calcutta Cup so soon in the offing. Eventually, only Steve McDowell, Frano Botica and Kieran Crowley took part. I was selected on the left wing to oppose Ian Williams and it was a pretty disappointed Rory Underwood who shook me by the hand and wished me well. It was a close fought encounter, which both sides regarded as an unofficial fourth Test, and we came away with a 19–15 win.

The postscript to what had been a marvellous tour involved the secret machinations to get a World XV into South Africa to help celebrate the South African Rugby Board's centenary. Some went, others didn't and I was one of those who didn't go.

There was also a plan to take a British Isles XV to play in Paris as part of the French Republic's bicentennial celebrations. We had agreed as a squad not to go unless we could be accompanied by wives and girlfriends. Eventually, when the invitation came through, I decided that I would go after all. Fin and David Sole stuck to their guns and refused the invitation. The Lions did play in Paris for the first time and I am glad that I went. The split within the Lions ranks did cause some resentment at the time but not to the extent that it did any lasting damage to the strength of purpose and unity which had seen us travel the length and breadth of Australia and record 11 wins from our 12-match schedule. It was an honour and a privilege to have been part of it all.

7

A Wounded Lion

GEOFF COOKE, who was to manage the 1993 British Lions in New Zealand, was holding forth on BBC *Rugby Special* and I liked what I was hearing. I had played for the Scotland A side against Italy A at The Greenyards. We hadn't played particularly well. In fact we had struggled through to win by the slender margin of 22–17 but I was happy enough with my personal contribution and, judging from his comments on the box, Cooke – who had been at the game – had been reasonably impressed too.

I felt that my card had been marked and from then on I was hopeful that I would be on the plane as a double Lion when the squad left for New Zealand in that summer of 1993. But my hopes suffered a setback during the Five Nations campaign when I damaged ankle ligaments in the final game against England. However, my problems were insignificant when compared to those of Craig Chalmers who sustained a double-fracture of the arm in the same game and he was out for the duration. Similarly, Gary Armstrong, who would certainly have gone to New Zealand with the Lions as first-choice scrum-half, never recovered in time from a serious groin injury and he, too, found himself out of the reckoning. That's the thing about rugby. You can be riding along on the crest of the most fantastic wave and, in a trice, your luck has changed and you are on the sidelines. It can be a tough old sport.

Again, throughout the championship season which precedes a Lions tour, the thought is always there at the back of your mind that you are playing not just for your country but for a place with the Lions as summer approaches.

My main rivals, as I saw them, were once again Jeremy Guscott and Will Carling who had enjoyed an outstanding championship season. It seemed that they would be going to New Zealand, basically, as first-choice centres and I would be competing for a place with Ireland's Vinny Cunningham and Philip Danaher plus Mike Hall and Scott Gibbs from Wales. I had played alongside Graham Shiel for Scotland that championship season. Because he was a relative newcomer, he might have been considered last in the pecking order but he could by no means be discounted from the equation. There was certainly a lot of competition but I was still desperately keen to go to New Zealand.

The ankle ligaments damaged at Twickenham took about a month to heal which was perfect timing for the Lions. There had been much speculation first of all about who was going to captain the tourists. The two principal contenders were Gavin and Will Carling. Obviously, my money was on Gavin and I got an early nod from him that he had, indeed, got the job.

The manner in which the Lions' management went about the captaincy was as follows. First of all Gavin took a phone call from Ian McGeechan – who was to coach the tourists – asking if he would like to be captain. Gav said that, of course, he would love to do the job. Then, there was a second phone call from Cooke about half an hour later in which Gavin was told that the job was his.

The squad was due to be announced the following day but, as Gavin was speaking to Geoff, he decided to ask whether I was in or not. He was sworn to secrecy but was told that I was in. I was working down in the Lake District that weekend and, when I phoned home to speak with Jenny she told me that I should phone the folks as they had something to tell me. When I did so I could hear the champagne corks popping in the background. Gavin came on the phone to congratulate me on my selection. So, with me now sworn to secrecy as well, I had a few pints of 'secret' Guinness at the Ullswater Outward Bound Centre, where I had been involved in running a team-building course with one of Barker's clients, Shell UK Exploration and Production. I was desperate to get back home to share my news and when I did so Jenny said that I was to go and see my parents. By the time I had returned home Jenny had organised an impromptu party at her parents' place with over 50 friends in attendance. She had put it all together within 24 hours. Ronnie Browne from The Corries was there singing away and the beer, buffet and celebrations went on long into the night.

So far as the controversy over the captaincy is concerned, I am obviously biased in favour of Gavin, but looking at the thing dispassionately I have no doubt that Gav was the correct choice. Carling had been the most successful captain in the history of the English game but in Gavin's favour was the fact that he had unparalleled experience of Kiwi rugby. He had been there with Scotland during the 1987 World Cup and had remained to play for Auckland University and had sat on the bench for the Auckland province. He had also been there with Scotland in 1990 and that experience was crucial in terms of knowing how the New Zealand rugby public and media behaved. There is, too, the fact that Gavin was always going to get more out of the Scottish, Welsh and Irish contingent than Will would ever have done. As a Scot, he was also much more liked by the New Zealand public than Carling the Pom was, and every little advantage that you can give yourself in the hostile environment of New Zealand rugby is going to stand you in good stead.

The fact that Gavin had succeeded and Carling had been overlooked seemed to impinge upon their relationship while we were on tour. Gavin was close to McGeechan while Carling was closer to Geoff Cooke and there was always a little bit of uneasiness so far as the two national captains were concerned.

Fellow Scots on tour were Kenny Milne, Paul Burnell, Andy Reed, Damian Cronin, Andy Reed and Peter Wright, who had enjoyed a good domestic season having first been capped on the 1992 Australia tour, but he was always treated by some in New Zealand as a player who did not really merit his place. The English contingent considered that their tight-head Jeff Probyn should have been there. The Dundee HS FP scrum-half Andy Nicol joined the party later to cover for Robert Jones who was suffering from tonsillitis. He got on for seven minutes during the 49–25 victory over Taranaki and achieved British Lions status after a remarkably rapid rise to top-flight rugby.

Four years down the line from the trip to Australia there were some new faces on board and it was clear that we faced a much tougher campaign in New Zealand than we had done in Oz.

We faced a tremendously tough schedule and after a week's preparation at Piahia in the beautiful Bay of Islands we were into action against North Auckland at Whangarei. I was delighted, just as I had been in 1989, to take part in the opening match which would set the trend for what was to come. Again, I partnered Jeremy Guscott in the centre and we achieved a workmanlike 17–30 victory which was marred by an injury to right wing Ian Hunter who dislocated a shoulder and that was him out of the tour. After all the training and preparation which he had put in he was on a flight back home within a couple of days. That's how cruel touring can be. Whangarei is Going territory and no North Auckland or Northland side is considered complete unless there are at least a couple of relatives of the former All Black scrum-half Sid Going on parade. There were three in the North Auckland side that Saturday and, unbelievably, Charles Going, who played in the centre, had played in opposition to Ian McGeechan when he had been out with the 1977 Lions.

After that game I noted in my diary: 'Getting to know how Jerry Guscott and Stuart Barnes play is half the battle. Jeremy jumps from one mood to another. He can be a most unsettling character. Even in training he will query whether Geech has called the right move and in a game if things haven't gone right, or if he gets a bad pass, then he just doesn't speak to you! But that's just Jeremy.'

I was on the bench for the next game against North Harbour which the Lions won 29–13 and in my diary I declare: 'A good performance, probably better than Saturday's. A 15–6 half-time lead was pulled back to 15–13 after some questionable refereeing. The spirit of the Lions pulled us through and we had tries from Ieuan Evans and Richard Webster. Tony Underwood scored a cracker which was the try of the game when he beat Eric Rush on the outside and kicked ahead to outstrip the defence. The match was held at the Mount Smart Stadium in Auckland where the 1990 Commonwealth Games were staged. We've had a good start to the tour with two wins out of two.'

We next flew to Wellington where the NZ Maoris lay in wait. The great thing about touring is that you bump into some of the game's great legends and our liaison officer in Wellington was All Black great Bernie Fraser. Richard Webster told Bernie that what he had admired him most for was his amazing moustache and that when the

All Blacks had toured Wales Richard had been a ball-boy at Swansea. Bernie, as sanguine a liaison man as he had been a player, didn't seem much impressed.

That game against the Maoris was incredible. I was playing alongside Will Carling on this occasion and I will never forget looking up at the Athletic Park scoreboard at half-time and it read 'NZ Maoris 20, British Isles 0'. We were in deep trouble. At training we had spent ages working on a couple of moves which we called Harlequins 1 and Harlequins 2. They involved mis-moves in the centre. Peter Winterbottom would go to deck and for '1' the ball would move right and for '2' it would go in the opposite direction. It was all about the angle and timing of the run between myself and Winterbottom. Ten minutes into the second half, with the sun and the slope in our favour, it began to come right and we started to put some points on the board. To come back from 20–0 down to win by 24–20 was a marvellous achievement but we had been sailing pretty close to Wellington's infamous wind. I was unhappy with my performance and I noted: 'I'll need to play a lot better than this if I'm to merit a Test place. The great thing about touring, though, is that you have the time and the opportunity to learn and get better and I will.'

The Maoris had given us quite a scare and, just as all Northern Hemisphere sides touring in New Zealand do, we were taking some time to come to terms with the refereeing. Refs seemed oblivious to the sight of players handling the ball on the deck in such a blatant manner that it would have been an immediate penalty back home. This was one facet of the game that we really concentrated on as we trained in preparation for the game against Canterbury. We trained at Leestown RFC and afterwards the ladies of the club treated us to a feast of mince and tatties. Now, this might sound rather mundane but when you are on tour, eating hotel food all the time, it is a rare pleasure and delight to be able to sit down to some good, old-fashioned home cooking. Strange, isn't it, the kind of things that stick in the mind.

Kenny Milne organised some ten-pin bowling for the squad and it was deemed to be compulsory. 'Do we have to go?' asked Nick Popplewell who was one of the stars of the trip, both in his deeds on the park and in his off-duty roles as Father Popplewell – father confessor to the tour party – and as the Lion responsible for seeking out the Guinness pubs wherever we happened to be.

We had a solid 28–10 win over Canterbury in Christchurch when I was on bench duty and, even at this early stage in the tour, it was becoming clear that, whereas in the past it had been Lions packs which had laid the foundations for victory, we were relying much more this time on the enterprising play of the backs.

Next up were Otago at Carisbrook in Dunedin. This was being billed as a 'shadow' Test and I note from my diary that I was bitterly disappointed not to have been selected. I didn't know it at the time but even greater disappointment was lying in wait for me in the Edinburgh of the Southern Hemisphere. Carling and Guscott had been selected as the centres. Jeremy had, in my opinion, already played himself into contention for the first Test which was but a week away and I was battling for a berth against Carling and Scott Gibbs. Will was playing poorly and I reckoned I was ahead of him in the pecking order. I was, though, concerned and decided to have a word with Gavin. Gav was in an awkward position and he couldn't really tell me too much about what was happening on the selection front but he just told me to keep playing away and doing my talking on the field. Although I was on the bench against Otago there was still Southland to play before the Test side was due to be selected. I was confident of being chosen to play against Southland in Invercargill and I believed that my Test aspirations were still very much alive.

We had a few hours to kill in the days before the game in Dunedin so Mick Galwey, Paul Burnell, Damian Cronin, Kenny Milne and I headed off to an indoor go-kart track. We enjoyed it so much that the entire party put in a block booking for the following day. However, Geoff Cooke found out about it and the outing was banned. However, not to be completely thwarted in our social aspirations, we headed out that night to Rosie O'Grady's, yet another Irish pub where Mad Mick and Father Popplewell were the Celtic masters of ceremony.

Otago were fielding a strong side against the Lions – to name but a few, John Timu, Mark Ellis, Steve Bachop, Stu Forster, Jamie Joseph, Arran Peni and a young flanker named Josh Kronfeld whom I was soon to get to know at extremely close quarters and who would, of course, go on to be one of the All Black stars in the 1995 World Cup.

My diary takes up the story: 'Saturday, 5 June – a day I am not going to forget in a hurry. I was sitting on the bench and, for some reason, I knew that I was going to get on. While we were walking around on the pitch before kick-off one of the Carisbrook seagulls landed one on my head. I was covered in the stuff. It's supposed to be lucky. The boys told me I would definitely get a game. Nine minutes into the game Carling got carted and I could see the door of opportunity opening. I reckoned that if I got on to the pitch a week before the Test then I had a golden opportunity to stake a claim for a Test spot.'

Well, opportunity was knocking for someone but it definitely wasn't me. Carling had strained a leg muscle and as he was limping off I was determined to seize my chance with both hands. I now had everything to play for. I didn't know the extent of Carling's injury and, who knows, he might not even have been fit for selection for the first Test.

The Lions had been playing some magnificent rugby but, on the stroke of half-time, Otago created a try from nothing and scored at the other end to make it 13–18 at the turn. They had been very physical and, as the second half got under-way, it was clear that with Bachop as the catalyst they really had their backs up. Then in the 47th minute the sky fell in on me and I was out of the tour.

We were defending inside our 22. Bachop threw a looping pass to Kronfeld and I went full bore to hit him in the tackle. As I ducked in to make the hit I caught his knee full in the face. I must have been instantaneously knocked out because when I came around I tried to close my mouth but it wouldn't shut properly. My first thought was that the jaw was broken. I knew something major was wrong and I stood straight up and walked off the pitch.

While I was down hurt Otago had scored and it was only when the Lions were behind the posts waiting for the conversion attempt that they realised I was missing. Gavin had been looking for me and somebody told him that I was off. I was very dazed and as I came off the pitch James Robson, the doctor, and the physio Kevin Murphy both ran towards me. The look on James's face suggested that something was badly amiss.

By this stage I felt as though the side of my head had caved in. There wasn't much pain, just a dull ache which was telling me that I had to keep my head as still as possible. Unbelievably, the New

Zealand doctor who was responsible for sanctioning the replacement, asked me if I wanted to go back on. I murmured that I would rather not!

A quick look in the mirror told me that the cheekbone had gone. I burst into tears, not because of the pain, but because I knew my tour was over and all the effort and sacrifice had been for nothing. The emotion was just too much. James confirmed that the cheekbone was fractured but, at that stage, he couldn't say whether or not there was a problem with the jaw as well.

I was taken off to hospital in a taxi with our liaison man David Johnston looking after me. I was dumbstruck that such a thing could have happened. By this time the pain was much more severe. Each time I moved a searing pain seemed to shoot through my entire head. By the time we reached the hospital I was on the point of collapse and couldn't speak. A young nurse told me to lie down on a bed and she gave me a shot of morphine. That was pure bliss.

Strangely, once the drug had taken the pain away, I found myself lying in the accident and emergency department working out my schedule for the following season. Right there and then, as I was waiting for the medics to come and take me to the operating theatre, I had decided that I would stay in New Zealand to watch the first Test. Then, in a panic almost, I thought that I would have to get a phone message to Jenny letting her know that I was hurt but I was all right. I thought with horror about her getting word that I was seriously hurt in the middle of the Scottish night. Next, in my drug-induced and almost euphoric state, I decided that I had to make sure that I would be fit in time to play against the All Blacks at Murrayfield in five months' time and that I had to have a successful season in 1994. Once all that had been sorted out to my satisfaction I just lay there contentedly and waited for the medics to get to work.

An x-ray examination confirmed that the cheekbone was broken and that there were two hairline fractures of the upper jaw. Back at Carisbrook the Lions had lost 37–24 and James Robson arrived at the hospital with the good news that they had managed to phone Jenny and bring her up to date with what had happened. Within three hours of arriving in hospital I was in the operating theatre and the surgeons worked on me for just short of four hours during which time they inserted a plate and pinned the jaw in place. My teeth were wired together and my mouth had to remain closed for a week during which time I fed myself through a straw.

Throughout that first night I had to be woken every hour just to make sure that I was OK and my recollection is that I seemed to spend most of the time signing autographs for the young nurses! The surgeons and everybody else involved had done a wonderful job. They were all rugby daft and as a wounded Lion I was being treated like a lord.

The following morning Gavin, Ian McGeechan and James Robson came round to see me. There had been a party in the team hotel the night before – a party which I had helped to organise. Gavin had obviously enjoyed himself and when he first caught sight of me in the hospital bed he almost brought up his breakfast!

I was trying to put a brave – if battered and bruised – face on it but, really, I felt desperately sorry for myself. It was a bummer. By my reckoning I had been close to Test selection but now I was going to have to leave the camaraderie of the tour and would soon be on my way home.

Martin Bayfield had suffered a potentially serious neck injury in the same game. I was out and Carling was also hurt. Then, when the squad travelled down to Invercargill leaving me behind in Dunedin, word came through that Wade Dooley's father had died and that he would be returning home for the funeral. The Lions' problems were certainly mounting up and with the Test less than a week away it represented something less than the ideal preparation.

My diary for Sunday, 6 June, records: 'I got out of hospital this afternoon. I was collected by Ruth, an assistant manager from the team hotel. We went for a walk down to one of the local beaches. It was a beautiful day but, boy, was I down. The hotel was empty. The boys had all moved on. Jack from Kilmarnock rugby club tried to cheer me up and we had a few beers to help him celebrate his birthday. Drinking is OK but eating presents a major problem! I freshened myself up with a bath – my first since Friday – and I phoned Jenny for some cheering up. I'm looking forward to seeing her and Corey again.'

That was the last entry in the tour diary. That evening I went down to the hotel restaurant to have some soup. I was the only Lion left on the premises. When I walked in, giving a more than adequate performance as John Merrick, the elephant man, all eyes turned in my direction. I was in a sorry state. I had a couple of mouthfuls of soup and went back to my room. There can be nothing worse than being alone and injured on the other side of the world. I returned to the hospital on the Monday for a check-up and they told me that the operation had gone well and that there were no problems. They faxed all the details of the operation back to Donald Macleod, the SRU doc at Murrayfield, so that they would be up to speed for my post-operative treatment, and I made ready to get myself down to Invercargill to meet up with the tour party once again.

The Lions hit more injury problems against Southland when Stuart Barnes came off with a horrific head cut which more or less ruled him out of contention for Test selection. Ironically, he had come by the cut after he had gone on, like me, as a replacement. Rob Andrew had suffered a broken nose when he was caught at the bottom of a ruck and, with just ten minutes left on the clock, Barnes had gone on to replace him. He lasted nine minutes and the Lions finished the match with both fly-halves on the casualty list and Dewi Morris filling in as an impromptu stand-off. The bench was turning out to be a pretty dangerous place to be on this tour!

Arrangements were made for me to fly home after the first Test in Christchurch. In the meantime I was still with the squad but feeling very much surplus to requirements. Things became so bad that I fell into bad company with the Press men who were following the trip! After one eight-pint afternoon in Lochinvar's, a Christchurch bar, I made my way back to the hotel for a team meeting during which I fell asleep and began snoring heavily. Thereafter, I decided that I would be as well keeping out of the team's way. The Test was looming and they didn't need the distraction of a mellow S. Hastings keeping them from the task in hand.

The Test itself was one of the cruellest games of rugby that I have ever witnessed. The Lions had played outstandingly well and with just a minute to go they were leading 18–17. Dean Richards tackled Frank Bunce near our ten-metre line. The ball came out our way and Dewi Morris had it in his hands when the Australian referee Brian Kinsey, inexplicably, blew his whistle for a penalty against the Lions. Grant Fox kicked the goal and the Lions lost 20–18. I have never been in a changing-room where there was a mood of such utter desolation. The Lions had played their hearts out. They had managed to recover from a dubious All Black try early on and the game had been theirs until Kinsey intervened.

It was, though, time for me to go. On the day following the Test Graham Pittman, who had toured with Watsonians in the early '80s and who now lives in Nelson, took me to a rugby league game. We drank a lot of beer that afternoon and evening and the next day I was on the plane for a long and very sad flight home.

Thereafter, my role was the same as that of thousands of other rugby fans who got up in the middle of the night to watch the rest of the Lions' campaign on television. Their second Test victory, by the convincing margin of 20–7, was superb and recompense in part for the manner in which they had been robbed of a win in the first encounter. There had been great doubt surrounding Gavin's fitness for the second Test. He had tweaked a hamstring and didn't want to play because he didn't want to let anyone down.

However, Ian McGeechan had encouraged Gavin to get on the field. Geech had said to him that he meant so much to the Lions that he wanted him in the starting line-up. I can't speak highly enough of the manner in which Gavin led that Lions party. He was well respected by every member of the squad and respected, too, by the New Zealanders – players and public.

Looking on from afar, one of the saddest aspects of the tour as it reached the latter stages, was how poorly the mid-week team performed. They lost to Hawkes Bay 29–17 and, 38–10 to Waikato when they were totally outplayed There just didn't seem to be any spirit to them. I'm sure that those involved will deny this but, to me, it seemed that they had thrown in the towel. They played like men who had given up all hope of being promoted or re-promoted to the Test side. Sadly, I have to include in that category many of my Scotland colleagues. I don't know what went wrong, particularly against Waikato, but the one Lion whom I absolve from that collective stupor is Will Carling. Despite the fact that he had lost his Test place, the England captain continued to play with pride and determination but he is about the only one that you could say that about. It is so very important when you are away that the mid-week side performs to the best of its ability. The reasons are two-fold. Firstly if the mid-weekers are performing well then that maintains the competition for Test places. Secondly, victories gained in mid-week relieve much of the pressure on the Saturday side which, traditionally, plays the strongest opposition. With the Lions in Australia in 1989, much of the success of the trip was down to the fact that Donal's Doughnuts played so well in the mid-week matches.

The All Blacks achieved a 2–1 series win after their 30–13 victory in the final Test before which they had obviously done their homework on the Lions. Life is full of 'if onlys', and in the final reckoning they count for nothing, but if only that opening Test had gone the way that it should have done then the Lions would, I am sure, have returned from New Zealand with a series win under their belts. The Lions had, just as the commemorative book produced afterwards records, come so close to glory. With the professional game in a state of flux there may never be a next time. Let's hope, though, that even in a professional game there will still be room for the British Lions. World rugby just wouldn't be the same without their historic and proud roar.

8

Black Saturday

On a Wing and a Prayer

THE TELEPHONE rang at about 11 o'clock on the Saturday night after Scotland's A side had played so well against Sean Fitzpatrick's New Zealanders at Old Anniesland in Glasgow.

I recognised the voice straight away. It was Scottish Rugby Union secretary and chief executive Bill Hogg. 'Congratulations, Scott. You've been selected to play for Scotland against New Zealand at Murrayfield next Saturday. You'll be playing on the left wing,' said Bill.

Initially, I thought that he was joking. 'You're winding me up, Bill,' I said. 'No, no, you've been selected to play on the wing and we look forward to seeing you at training later in the week,' he replied.

'But Bill . . . ' I stammered. 'No, Scott. We're sure you'll do very well. You've got experience on the wing haven't you? You've played there for the British Lions.'

'Yes,' I said, ' but that was four years ago against the ANZACS in 1989. That was the last time that I played on the wing. You can't really be serious. How can they expect me to play on the wing in an international against the All Blacks when I haven't played there for four seasons and God knows when before that?'

The conversation fizzled out when Bill said that he would have to make calls to the rest of the team. It wasn't Bill's fault. He hadn't played any part in selection. Normally a call from the secretary meant good news. It meant you were in the side. This time, though, I was seriously concerned by his news.

I turned to Jenny and told her what had just taken place. 'I cannot believe this. They've selected me on the wing to play against the All Blacks,' I said.

I was so unsettled that I didn't sleep a wink that night. I had established myself as a Scotland centre where I had played 46 times and, now, without any consultation, I was being switched to the wing.

The following day I received a telephone call from coach Douglas Morgan. By this time I had, of course, discovered that the centre combination was to be Ian Jardine, winning his first cap, and Graham Shiel. I said that Ian hadn't played outside centre at any level for at least a couple of seasons. Dougie assured me that he had and that he had actually been playing a combination of left and right for Stirling and Glasgow.

Because the selectors had waited until they had seen how the A side had got on against the Kiwis before naming the side, there was less than a week to go before the game and we met as a squad on the Tuesday before the match for the first time. I asked Jardie – who was obviously immensely pleased to have been selected for his first cap – if he had been playing outside centre lately. He said the last time he had done so had been over two seasons ago.

There had obviously been some breakdown in communication. Dougie must have been watching the wrong Ian Jardine playing outside centre for Stirling County. However, I had to accept the decision and although I was filled with a deep sense of foreboding about being played out of position, I was still keen to tilt the lance at the All Blacks. That summer I had been out in New Zealand with the British Lions and had come home early after suffering a serious facial injury. I had been desperately keen to win a Lions' Test place against the New Zealanders and, while the injury was healing, had consoled myself by thinking that at least I would have another chance when they came to Scotland in the autumn.

The build-up to the game went as well as any in which I have been involved. I consider it a great honour to be picked for Scotland and despite my huge misgivings I was reconciled to playing on the wing against a golden-haired youngster by the name of Jeff Wilson who had just turned 20 and who would be winning his first cap.

Coming together on the Tuesday instead of the more usual Thursday had allowed us two extra days in which to prepare. As I've said, it went well but with the benefit of hindsight it is possible to identify at least some of the reasons why it all went horribly wrong.

Murrayfield stadium was undergoing the final phase of its reconstruction. The old West Stand had been demolished so the ground was enclosed on three sides only. There was a ramshackle, makeshift hut for the dignatories to sit in where the magnificent West Stand had been and a building site behind. The teams got changed in two marquees erected on the back pitches and had to walk through the debris left from the demolished stand to get to the ground. When you consider how important the crowd and the atmosphere has been to Scottish teams at Murrayfield over the years you can imagine how bizarre this situation was.

It was, of course, the same for the New Zealanders, but through the '80s and into the '90s Scotland had become used to the very special atmosphere which greeted us at Murrayfield. It was almost like an extra man. There had been some speculation as to whether the SRU might take the game to Ibrox Stadium, the Rangers FC ground in Glasgow, and now I very much wish that the union had grasped this superb marketing opportunity rather than insisting that the game went ahead on the Murrayfield building site.

Two days before the game Craig Chalmers had pulled up at training with a calf muscle injury. He was a doubtful starter but the medics got him sorted out with an anti-inflammatory jab – and what a fuss that was to cause later – but in all probability he should not have played because he was hampered by the injury and had to go off with less than an hour played.

Gavin also had to go off, temporarily, with a bad cut to a thumb; Damian Cronin, who was palpably unfit to play, was replaced by Carl Hogg of Melrose; and Andy Nicol had to go off for running repairs when Bryan Redpath came on for a 60-second cap. There was so much coming and going that Murrayfield was looking like Waverley Station at the rush-hour. The whole afternoon was such an appalling débâcle that, even now, I can barely bring myself to talk about it.

For me the game began badly and got worse. Much, much worse. It was my mistake which let golden-bollocks Wilson in for the first of his three tries. I've watched it since on video and there's no doubt that Frank Bunce sent Wilson in for his first Test try with a forward pass but I should have stayed on Wilson and didn't.

As the game wore on and the score mounted – 0–3, 0–8, 3–8,

3–15, 6–15, 6–22, 9–22 at half-time – more and more tackles were missed and New Zealand just ground us into the Murrayfield turf. By full-time we had suffered a record 51–15 defeat and it was the most humiliating day of my life. I was trying my heart out on the wing but I felt totally naked and exposed. The atmosphere, or lack of it, was surreal. I had let Wilson in for a try in the first few minutes. He had then gone in for another and then a third which he also converted to give him a tally of 17 points on his international debut.

The New Zealanders played very, very well but we played so poorly that even now I still can't believe it. The biggest cheer of the day came when New Zealand got their half century. I walked from the pitch utterly dejected. It was a sense of complete and utter desolation. It was the lowest of the lows in my rugby career and, from a selectorial point of view, it was the lowest of the lows as well. To this day the selectors have never admitted that they got it wrong.

I sat in the changing-tent afterwards and reflected on such a poor personal performance. Dougie Morgan patted me on the back, with the comment, 'That's Test match rugby'. That didn't go down well with me at all. I was furious, embarrassed and distraught that we had let Scotland down. I was angry with myself over my performance but angrier still with the selectors who had put me in that position. I had felt woefully exposed in front of 50,000-plus people. I didn't know what angles I was supposed to be running in defence and attack – not that we did much of the latter – and was just so much out of position. Ian Jardine confided that he, too, had felt uneasy about the unaccustomed role he was playing at outside centre.

Scotland is such a small rugby-playing nation that we have to play to our strengths all the time and one of my strengths has always been the solidity that I bring to the midfield. Yet there I was, against the world's top side, being played out of position and with one of the great selectorial cock-ups of all time being displayed for all to see. It is not an experience that I would care to repeat ever again.

But life has to go on and a fortnight later I was scheduled to face the All Blacks again with the Barbarians in Cardiff. On a previous Barbarians trip I had been dropping the heaviest of hints to Baa-Baas president Mickey Steele-Bodger that 4 December was an important day for me.

'What's particularly special about 4 December, Mickey?' I asked him.

'That's when we play New Zealand,' he said.

'What else?'

'Come on then, Scott. What else?' said a thoroughly bemused Baa-Baas' president.

'It's my birthday. What a birthday present it would be to play for you against the All Blacks,' I replied.

Mickey took the hint and a few weeks later the Barbarians' secretary Geoff Windsor-Lewis called to say that not only had I been selected but, because Gavin who was scheduled to captain the side was injured, they were going to make me captain as well.

'We reckon you'll be doing so much talking anyway that we might as well make you captain,' said Geoff.

So, I captained the Barbarians' side which played the All Blacks at the Arms Park in the final match of their tour. We lost 25-12 but it was a fantastic game of rugby in which Tony Clement had an outstanding game and in which Gary Armstrong made his return to top-grade rugby at scrum-half. I was performing in my normal centre berth and played well, so the scars inflicted at Murrayfield on Black Saturday, 20 November 1993, healed quicker than they would have done if I hadn't been given the opportunity to play against the New Zealanders again so soon. The scars have healed but they have left their mark. I shudder when I recall that match which saw Scottish rugby, and my own game, at their lowest ebb – an experience never, ever, to be repeated.

9

Old Farts and New Money

The Professional Revolution

THE REEK of revolution was in the air when the world's top players gathered in South Africa for the 1995 World Cup. Over 100 years of amateurism and shamateurism were careering to a messy end on the back of outright revolt in the Southern Hemisphere where the concept of amateurism had become a sick joke, as a result of the millions ploughed into the game in Australia, New Zealand and South Africa by Rupert Murdoch's News Corporation.

On the eve of the World Cup final in Johannesburg the chairman of the South African Rugby Football Union, Louis Luyt, revealed that the three Southern Hemisphere authorities had signed a £370million deal with Murdoch giving his News Corporation exclusive broadcasting rights for all top-grade rugby in the three countries.

The deal provided the impetus and the funding for a truly professional game and it was the threat of a professional breakaway by the three Southern Hemisphere giants which propelled the International Board to perform the death rites on amateurism at its historic meeting in Paris two months later. The IB had already carried out its own investigation into worldwide abuses of the amateur ethic and they had discovered what most of us already knew, which was that, to a hugely significant degree, the game had been professional in many parts of the world for years.

However, when it declared an 'open' game, the International Board had given little or no thought to how professional rugby would operate. They had grasped the nettle of professionalism and, in the same moment, cast it aside. They failed miserably to set in place a structure in which the transition from amateurism or shamateurism to full-blooded professionalism could take place. Again, the IB members had shown that they were not in control of events. They were reactive and not pro-active. They had acted only because of the Southern Hemisphere threat and had displayed yet again their inability to govern efficiently the game which they are supposed to administer on our behalf.

This failure to set in place a structure in which a global professional game could prosper created a void into which stepped an Australian entrepreneur by the name of Ross Turnbull. He had a plan and a structure and, he said, the money to transform rugby almost overnight into a truly global, major professional sport. The story about how close he and his associates came to winning control of the world-wide game – and specifically how close he came to buying up virtually the whole of the Scottish international squad – represents a lesson for rugby's administrators in the folly of leaving a job half done. The England captain Will Carling might have chosen his words with more eloquent care when he dismissed the Rugby Football Union committee as a collection of 'Old Farts' but the sentiment is one with which few players would disagree.

I cannot see a future in the new era for a game run by committee. The RFU and the SRU and all the other organisations which are supposedly in charge of the game will have to get themselves up to speed very quickly and that means in Scotland that there is no place for an 18-man committee which has to sanction every little thing which the union wants to do. The game, which is now a multi-million pound business, should be run by an executive committee and a chief executive who can make immediate tactical and strategic decisions without having to wait for another monthly committee cycle to grind around.

However, I'm galloping off on a hobby-horse when what we should be focusing upon is the grand plan which the Sydney lawyer and one-time ARFU administrator Ross Turnbull put into operation in the late summer of 1995. It was as simple as it was audacious.

The first-class game could not operate without the leading players and so he and his lieutenants set about buying up the world's top 1000 players. Once the players had signed, Turnbull would then be in a position to realise his World Rugby Corporation dream of a series of global competitions within a professional structure and, if necessary, the game could be franchised on a national basis to the existing administrations in each country.

Almost as soon as the World Cup was over Turnbull set to work. Bankrolled, it was said, by Australian media mogul Kerry Packer, who just happens to be Rupert Murdoch's arch-rival, he contacted leading players in every major rugby-playing nation and they became his recruiting sergeants. The involvement of the Springbok captain Francois Pienaar has been well documented. He had obtained signed contracts for World Rugby Corporation from virtually every member of South Africa's World Cup winning squad. Similar recruitment drives went on in New Zealand, Australia and everywhere else where top rugby was played.

But Pienaar never handed the signed documents to WRC and Turnbull's plan began to unravel in South Africa when the South African Rugby Football Union, which had, of course, already struck its deal with News Corporation, used a combination of cash and threats to get their players back on side. The affair ended in court and Turnbull's coup was beginning to fall apart. Almost simultaneously, Australian and New Zealand players who had been in the WRC fold began to have second thoughts and with the promise of seriously lucrative contracts from their own unions, they, too, began to abandon the Turnbull ship.

But what has not been fully appreciated until now is that in Scotland, too, the Ross Turnbull coup came within a whisker of succeeding.

After the World Cup, Turnbull and his associate, Michael Hill of the Turnbull–Hill partnership based in Charleston, New South Wales, were in contact with my brother Gavin in an effort to determine whether or not he considered their WRC concept worthwhile.

Gavin had just retired from international rugby after leading Scotland at the World Cup and was in the process of setting up in business in his own right with Hastings International, his sports marketing company. He was recruited as the go-between and agreed to make contact with the squad which had just returned from South Africa.

Gavin thought that the Turnbull–Hill plan was worthy of consideration because he felt, as we all did, that the International

Board had more or less thrown the game to the wolves by their failure to provide a framework in which professionalism could prosper. He spent many hours talking to the players who had been with him in South Africa and, ultimately, 18 of the 26 players who had taken part in the World Cup signed up with World Rugby Corporation.

Before the WRC concept fell apart I had met Michael Hill, along with a number of my Scottish colleagues at a 'secret' meeting at Myreside. He had been offering two and three-year contracts worth in excess of £100,000 per season. It was a significant sum of money. The legal document declared that Turnbull's company proposed to transform rugby union and take it into a new and exciting era of professionalism while attempting to protect its history and traditions.

My contract stated: 'Subject to the organisation going ahead the company agrees to pay you a contract fee of $115,000. Your two-year service contract provides a payment from the company of $175,000 per year.' The agreement included a cast-iron confidentiality clause which meant that, at the time, none of the players who had signed could talk openly about it. Basically, I was just going with the flow. If it all worked out then I was going to be earning some serious money after a lifetime in the game when I had made huge sacrifices for little or no financial reward. If it didn't then nothing had been lost.

There were flaws in the contract, such as the stipulation that if you were not selected for your national franchise – in our case Scotland – then you could be sent to represent one of the franchises in another country. But we were willing to take a gamble. What we wanted to do was to play rugby against the best players in the world and if they were with Turnbull then we would have to go with him as well. After the deal fell through following the re-defection of the Southern Hemisphere players, Turnbull still had contact with a large number of top players, including those from Scotland and the other Five Nations competitors, and there was then a second attempt to set up a professional game based in Europe. He wanted to establish a European Championship involving players from Scotland, England, Ireland, Wales, France and Italy. In Scotland, because at this time there were no contracts with the Scottish Rugby Union, we feared that if Turnbull's European Championship got off the ground then there was a very real chance that we would be left behind. If the top players in the other nations had signed, then, basically, there would be nobody left for us to play against and so most of us threw in our lot with Turnbull and his new plan. Again, most of the Scottish international squad were involved, although Gavin declined on the basis that he had retired from the game and was concentrating on developing his business interests.

The cash for the European deal was significantly less – £40,000-plus a season for two seasons – and Turnbull was talking about sixteen teams competing in a European 'club' Championship. The plan was to put in place a Northern Hemisphere structure which would rival that which existed in the Southern Hemisphere thanks to the Murdoch money. The teams would play on a home and away format, followed by an end-of-season six-nations cup for international sides also to be played on a home and away basis. In the 'club' competition there would be six representatives from England, four from Wales, three from France, and one apiece from Scotland, Ireland and Italy.

All of the top English and Welsh clubs had also been approached by Turnbull and it had been established that Scottish internationalists playing for Bath and Newcastle, and so on, would be made available for the Scotland team which would compete in the end-of-season six-nations cup. We would have been playing 30 games per season in the club championship and would then have had the international matches at the end so there was more than enough to keep us occupied.

The plan was that we would play throughout the 1996 Five Nations tournament and that Turnbull's European Championship concept would come into operation at the start of the 1997 season. We were led to believe that well over 100 of the top players in the UK had signed with Turnbull. The Welsh had taken little persuading, the French and Italians were on board, the English were – with hindsight – perhaps using the Turnbull plan as a negotiating lever with their own union and the Irish were dragging their feet.

Eventually, though, just like his attempt at a global coup, the concept fell apart. This time the problem was one of finance. Turnbull and Hill had been unable to get the necessary funding in place and in February, 1996 we received letters from Australia telling us that the deal was off and the contracts, which were held under lock and key by an Edinburgh solicitor, were to be destroyed. When I met Turnbull I was impressed by the vision which he had for the future of the game and particularly so because the kind of vision which he was bringing to bear upon professionalism was – and still is – absent from what was on offer from the International Board.

What he was offering, once we had returned from Scotland's tour to New Zealand, with a start on 1 September 1996, was a structure within which, as professional players, we could operate. A year and more on from the International Board's momentous decision in Paris, the game is still in a state of flux. There appears in the Northern Hemisphere to be no leadership, no vision and no focus on how the professional game is going to operate and prosper. In the Southern Hemisphere, meanwhile, the Super 12 and Tri-Nations series appears to have been a huge success.

If the IB had done its job properly then there would have been no window of opportunity for Ross Turnbull to clamber through. He might not have succeeded in what he was attempting to do but, at least, he had a vision, flawed though it was, for the future of the game which the IB has never come close to emulating.

If the deal had come off then it would have caused mayhem within the Scottish game and within the Scottish Rugby Union. The consequences for the SRU in terms of its sponsorship deals and so on would have been severe. Now, some people will no doubt, view us as a bunch of disloyal mercenaries but you have to look at the situation like this – the players didn't decide that the game was going to turn professional. That was the decision of the International Board, taken as I have said, against a backdrop of commercial pressures from the Southern Hemisphere. So as players we became, virtually overnight, professionals. When a situation was developing whereby the top 200 players in Britain were being approached with what seemed an incredibly attractive and plausible professional proposition we, in Scotland, just could not afford either in a playing or cash sense, to be left behind. I want to play rugby against top opposition just as I have done since 1986 and there was no way that I was wanting to be playing in any kind of second-rate competition when my colleagues and rivals from other countries had moved on to something entirely different.

There was also a sense, I admit, that somehow we were about to get what had been due to us for all those years of unpaid service to the cause. When we were out in South Africa for the World Cup one just had to look around the hundreds of hospitality suites at the Loftus Versfeld Stadium in Pretoria to realise that a great many people were making huge sums of money from the game and yet the players – the guys who actually made the blood, sweat and tears sacrifices and who saw family and business relationship suffer because of their commitment to the game – were receiving peanuts. That situation just could not continue any longer.

The period which followed the August 1995 declaration that amateurism was dead has been an immensely damaging one for the game as a whole. We have witnessed the clubs versus districts row in Scotland and we have seen the quite remarkable developments in England where the top clubs declared that they would not participate in any competitions organised by the Rugby Football Union.

We witnessed the disruption caused by the RFU's decision to negotiate its own Five Nations television deal with Sky television and the incredibly damaging uncertainty surrounding the future of the Five Nations official European Cup competition organised by the Five Nations' off-shoot, European Rugby Cup Ltd. In the Southern Hemisphere, where all seems to be sweetness and light since they did their deal with News Corporation, they must be laughing all the way to the bank.

Just about the same time as all of this was going on I was contacted by Leeds RFC with an invite to come on board as their director of rugby. They were offering £160,000 for a two-year contract. They were playing in the English fourth division but had hugely ambitious plans to fight their way to the top of the English game. That is an incredible sum of money to be offered virtually out of the blue but I was still hoping that the Turnbull plan for a European competition would bear fruit and the beauty of that was that I could earn some money from rugby and still remain in Edinburgh. I turned Leeds down and 24 hours later they appointed the Welsh internationalist Phil Davies and I hope he does well. I rather suspect that anyone who takes on the job of rugby director in the professional era will need all the luck that's going because there is no doubt in my mind that they will succeed or fail in direct proportion to their results on the field. If they lose too many games then, like football managers, they will be out. And in a game where there might only be 15–20 clubs paying full-time rugby directors, that means that their opportunity for manoeuvre and continuing employment is going to be strictly limited.

Money has never been the main motivating factor in my life. Away back in 1989 I was offered a deal worth £250,000 to sign for Bradford Northern. This had come on the back of the British Lions tour to Australia. I took a call at my office in Edinburgh from a chap called Chris Caisley who was a solicitor and a board member at Bradford.

He came up to see me and we had a long session in the Caledonian Hotel during which he put forward what seemed to be quite an exciting proposition. I turned them down and within 24 hours they had increased the offer to £275,000. However, it was only when I had looked closely at the smallprint that you began to realise that a rugby league offer of £275,000 is not all that it seems. There were subsidiary clauses which indicated that I would receive the full amount only if I played 50 games for the club and if I was selected for the international side and so on and so on. For that reason I was always suspicious whenever I read and heard of yet another Welshman taking the road north for yet another telephone-number fee.

Next, Hull Kingston Rovers were beating a path to my door in the form of one Max Gold. After quite a few telephone conversations I told Max that my ambition was to win the Grand Slam with Scotland. A couple of days after we did just that in 1990 Max was back on the telephone telling me he wished he had taken me at my word and that he had slapped a few hundred quid on Scotland. So he never got me and he missed out on a killing with Scotland as well.

The final attempt to lure me to rugby league came from Castleford and, I must say, I rather admired their straightforward approach. There must have been a lot of speculation at the time as to whether I was ripe for picking or not and when the phone rung on this occasion the caller identified himself as the Castleford coach.

'I'm sick of all this conjecture. I've only got one 10p for the phone so make it quick. Are you interested? Yes or no,' he said.

I said no. The phone went dead and I was troubled no more by rugby league.

It wasn't the game for me. I've no doubt that I could have adapted and could have done rather well at it but I just didn't like the game.

When we were out in Australia with Scotland in 1992 we had gone
to a couple of big-time rugby league matches and I was bored stiff.
The players are very fit and athletic. They give and take huge hits
and they handle extremely well but, too often its repetitive nature
has me reaching for the remote control. Rugby Union can learn a lot
from Rugby League, and the experiment at the tail end of the
1995–6 season, where Bath played Wigan at both codes, was
extremely revealing in terms of fitness, speed and strength.
Additionally, I have enjoyed the social side of rugby union. I have
made friends all over the world and I value, perhaps above all else,
that side of the game. I suspect that special camaraderie is sometimes
missing in rugby league and that is something which simply cannot
be bought.

10

The Hit Parade

MIDFIELD DEFENCE

DEFENCE HAS always been, in the eyes of many commentators, the strongest facet of my game. To an extent, this typecasting as a defensive midfield player irritates me because I feel that I have a lot to offer, too, in attack but I'm happy, nonetheless, to accept the plaudits for my defensive abilities.

I have always relished the physical side of rugby. Having been brought up with three brothers it was the rough and tumble aspect of the game which originally appealed to us. I got to grips with the technicalities of tackling very early on in my rugby education. Ian Gray, one of the schoolmasters at George Watson's College, was very particular that everybody under his care should be able to tackle properly and at least risk to themselves.

He stipulated a drill whereby we paired off and, with the tackler kneeling on the ground, we would go through the tackling routine of using, alternately, right and left shoulder to tackle on the hip while at the same time protecting your head on the cushion of your partner's buttock.

It was important to practise tackling with each shoulder because most players will favour one shoulder or the other. Being left-handed, my natural preference is for the left and, just as with most players who favour one foot or the other when kicking, regular practice with the 'unnatural' side should mean that the player is equally at ease with both. Similarly, during drills when we set up ruck and maul ball, I will use each shoulder alternately just to make sure that in a game situation, when you cannot predict whether it is better to 'tee up' the ball to left or right, I will be as proficient with one as with the other.

The physical side of the game is one which puts a lot of young players off and whenever I am invited to go along to a mini or midi coaching session I always make a point of pinpointing the youngster who obviously isn't relishing the tackling side of things. I then show them the tackling drill which Ian Gray used on me all those years ago as a means of demonstrating that tackling need not be a painful exercise so long as it is carried out in a technically correct manner. The key is to make sure that you get your head behind the opposing player and if you can get it on to the comfort zone of his backside then you shouldn't come to much harm.

Often, though, it is easier said than done and – as readers who have stuck with me this far in the book will have realised – I have on several occasions paid a hefty price for getting my head in the wrong place at the wrong time!

I have, though, been noted for the strength of my defence and it's certainly true that from a very early age I have taken great pride and pleasure whenever I have been able to stop an attacking player dead in his tracks. As I recount elsewhere, the special buzz which a good tackle gives me, arrived very early on in my career after I had seen the Welsh wizard Gerald Davies on TV pulling off a copybook diving tackle. I determined there and then that in my next game for George Watson's College junior school, I would emulate him. We were playing Morrison's Academy at Crieff when their winger escaped down the touchline. I raced after him and got within a couple of feet. It seemed that he was going to get away when I launched myself into the air and caught him around the bootlaces. He hit the deck like a felled tree and a certain try had been saved. I've always said, not entirely in jest, that it was the best tackle I ever made!

Specific tackles do stick in the mind, in the same way, I suspect, as a particular shot would remain in the memory of a golf pro. The tackle on Rory Underwood during the 1990 Grand Slam game is one which I relish. At that stage in the game we were operating a drift defence – and I'll explain later the kind of defensive strategies which are now part and parcel of an increasingly technical game – and as outside centre it was my role to hang back just a couple of yards from my inside man in case there was a move to bring in a

We have never all played together in the same team but three of us have, although, strangely, not for Watsonians. Ewan, Gavin and I played together for an outfit named the Quality Street Gang which is an incredibly select invitation side attached to York RFC. Following representations from the York president, Hugh Bowman, we play a charity match for the QSG once a season. Again, the Quality Street Gang strip is, like the Warblers, exotic in the extreme. The club colours are taken from the chocolate box of the same name and you can get QSG jerseys, ties, bow-ties, waistcoats, trousers and even kilts.

We felt that the annual charity game was a good opportunity to invite Ewan to come with us and he has a super photograph of him handing-off Simon Hunter, the great sevens exponent from Rosslyn Park. Ewan always excels with the Quality Street Gang and would invariably score a hat-trick of tries. They nicknamed him Rory Bremner because of his repertoire of impersonations. He would have them rolling in the aisles. Ewan thought it was because he was so good at his roll call of prime ministers and sporting personalities. Actually, it was because he was so appallingly bad. Don't give up the day job, Ewan. He plays on the wing in my invitation side because his great claim to fame is that, in his final year with the George Watson's College first XV, he was top try scorer. He reckons that he's just that bit faster than Gavin and me. No chance.

I've decided to select myself in my old Scottish Schoolboys' berth of fly-half, which means that there is a place in the centre for my Irish rival and British Lions colleague Brendan Mullin. He has been a great friend of mine since we captained our respective schools' sides in 1982. We suffered an absolute howkin' that day from a side which contained not only Brendan but Neil Francis and Terry Kingston plus quite a few others who went on to make their names in Irish senior rugby.

Since then, Brendan and I have played against each other on numerous occasions but in 1989 we were brothers in arms with the Lions in Australia and my touring destination with Brendan is the Queensland holiday resort of Cairns. We went there with the Lions for a brief spell of training away from the all-seeing eye of the Australian media but mainly for a spot of rest and recuperation when we scuba-dived off the Great Barrier Reef and did all the things that normal tourists do.

It was sublime and Brendan and I entered into the holiday spirit by attiring ourselves in sun shirts and Bermuda shorts. We found a great bar called Magnum's and while we sipped cool beers and melted into the background among the tourists and backpackers, Craig Chalmers and Robert Norster sauntered in dressed to the nines in full Lions' rig. They spotted us in our casual gear and beat a hasty retreat back to the Hilton Hotel where they changed and got more into holiday mood. After Magnum's, next stop was the Playpen where the wonderful Devils from Heaven, a Tasmanian rock band, were belting it out good and loud. They were followed by the Cairns wet T-shirt competition and we did our own spot of judging accompanied by a glass or three of Bundenberg rum – Australia's best. While we were in Cairns it became the tour drink and a Bundy on a Sunday was the order of the day. A great day, a better night and an interesting training session the following day!

Partnering Brendan in the centre is Sean Lineen who has been a great friend and Scotland colleague to me. Some of his greatest moments took place when we visited his second homeland, New Zealand, with Scotland in 1990.

Sean scored for Scotland against New Zealand in the first Test in Dunedin. It came off a move we called, appropriately enough, New Zealand 1. He looped me, romped in to score and the TV commentator blared out 'The Kiwi has scored against the Kiwis'. That was a proud day for Sean because he was as determined as anybody to get that elusive first win against New Zealand. By the time we went to New Zealand we had developed our relationship so well that we knew each other's play backwards. In the second Test, off a move we called New Zealand 2, I missed out Sean on a dummy run and passed straight to Gavin who cut inside John Kirwan and chipped the full-back Kevin Crowley, and Alex Moore, with his first touch in international rugby, was over for the try. That set us up nicely for one of the closest encounters we have ever had against New Zealand. We were kicked to death by Grant Fox and lost by the tantalising margin of 21–18.

That was the tour over but some of us decided to stay on for a few more days just to see a bit more of that beautiful country. Sean excelled himself. We had been to a winery – at which Kenny Milne asked what the oak casks were made of – and by the time we got back to Auckland we were feeling little pain. Sean 'mooned' across the main drag in Auckland before hailing a taxi with us in hot pursuit. Eventually Adam Buchanan-Smith and I tracked him down, and we decided to go to this bar which Sean had heard of called the Waterjump. En route, Sean stopped the taxi and disappeared into a store where he purchased a dozen eggs which were then ejected from our cab in the direction of unsuspecting passers-by and motorists. Sean, you would never get away with that in Edinburgh.

On the left wing is Iwan Tukalo and our destination is Hong Kong. After the 1990 Grand Slam, the Hawick flanker Derek Turnbull, Iwan, Gavin and I took ourselves off to the colony to play in the ten-a-side tournament which runs in tandem with the more famous sevens. We had a lot of fun. Our host was a splendid chap from Ardrossan RFC by the name of Jimmy Gibson, who is an architect out in Hong Kong. Our team was EATS – the Edinburgh Athenians Touring Society – which was a mix of Edinburgh Accies and Watsonians into which the four of us internationalists were shoe-horned. Actually, the playing side of the trip was rather embarrassing because we were knocked out in the quarter-finals through an inability to perform with alcohol in the system. We made up for it by being voted the best drinkers and the best singers the colony had ever seen.

We went out of the tournament on the Thursday and the following day we drowned our sorrows in quite spectacular fashion. There had been a dinner for all of the tens competitors on the Thursday night and Jimmy had to get us to the Hong Kong Hilton for lunch the following day where mine host was the Hilton's expat Scot manager James Smith and where the gathering was in honour of our sponsor Simon Murray of Hutchison-Wampoa. Jimmy was given the task of getting us to the lunch on time. In a moment of great wisdom, and before we had returned from dinner on the Thursday night, he pushed the clocks in our rooms forward by an hour.

We were, of course, an hour late by the time we got to the Hilton to meet our benefactor, but due to Jimmy's foresight we were in actual fact bang on time. That was just typical of Jimmy.

We sat down to lunch at about 12.30 and Simon left a couple of hours later after we had thanked him for flying us out and presented him with some Grand Slam memorabilia. We had been served the most magnificent meal, and somebody made reference to the fact that, really, coarse rugby players should not be drinking wine costing £80 a bottle, whereupon James Smith snapped his fingers, saying that was absolutely correct, and said these gentlemen should be drinking champagne at £120 a bottle. So out came the Dom Perignon, and very soon lunchtime had turned into tea-time and there was a procession of famous Scots to our table. Ian McGeechan looked in, as did Bill McLaren and many others whose faces, I fear, are now but a blur.

John Jeffrey was in town with the Scottish Border Club. He was staying in the hotel but couldn't be found and, as you do, we decided that if he couldn't be there in person then we would have to have an inflatable White Shark. James Smith snapped his fingers once again and, unbelievably, within 45 minutes an eight feet inflatable white shark had arrived at our table. The shark became the property of the Edinburgh Athenians Touring Society, and everywhere we then went in Hong Kong the shark was sure to go too.

We left the Hilton after darkness had fallen, and, courtesy of the Hilton's Daimler limo, we motored to Aberdeen Harbour and Lama Island. We found there a restaurant where the speciality of the house was pigeon, and we gorged ourselves on pigeon and beer for the rest of the evening.

Iwan and I commandeered a couple of bicycles for the down-hill trek from the restaurant to the jetty where we were to board the junk which was taking us back to Hong Kong. Even as I set this down on paper I still can't believe that it all actually happened. It was just one of those utterly bizarre days in the life of an international rugby player. Iwan set off first and I pedalled like fury to catch up. I turned a corner and there was Tooks and bike splattered all over the roadway. He had hit a rock and gone straight over the handlebars. But, just as he did on the rugby field, he shook himself like a wet dog and was up and back on to his bike in an instant. What a day, what a night. So Iwan and Hong Kong are indelibly etched on my memory.

I am at fly-half, and we'll decide later where my touring destination is to be, so I'll move on swiftly to our scrum-half who is going to be my best man and best schoolfriend Colin Hunter. He went on to play flanker in senior school and with the FPs, but in his early days he was a scrum-half so he'll not find his new role too awkward.

Colin, you will recall, was my partner in those games of gaining ground we used to play while we were youngsters at school. Our destination is Vancouver, where I had my first taste of the touring life with George Watson's College in 1980. That was where it all began. We were billeted with the parents of the boys we played against and it was fantastic. Colin and I shared a billet where our host was a young lady, who took us out on the town and we sampled a few illicit under-age beers. We went through the tour unbeaten and had a wonderful time. It was the camaraderie of touring that appealed to me and that is something which I've particularly cherished on every tour since. Colin is now in Melbourne, Australia, where he was married and my eldest brother Graeme was his best man. We got together during Scotland's tour to New Zealand in the summer of 1996 and it was great to see him again after so many years.

No rugby tour can be complete without visiting Dublin and that is a home-town destination for my loose-head prop Nick Popplewell. We were team-mates in New Zealand with the Lions in 1993 and got together again the following year when we were both selected to play for the Barbarians against South Africa at Lansdowne Road. That was just my second trip to Dublin outwith a Scotland context. The first time had been with Watsonians when we played in the Old Belvedere seven-a-side tournament. Our club dinner had taken place on a Friday night, and the following morning we flew out of Edinburgh for Dublin. Our visit coincided with the Eurovision Song Contest and although we weren't singing for Scotland we would have won hands down in any drinking contest. We had a superb Saturday night in Dublin's Fair City, so much so that I was forced to call an extra training session early the following morning. We just had to sweat some of the booze out of our systems, otherwise were were going to be in deep trouble once the tournament began. Rumours began spreading that those mad Scots had been so keen to do well that they had fitted in an extra session between 9 and 10 that morning. If only they had known the truth. Quite unbelievably, we went on to win the tournament and another fine old night was spent in the flesh-pots of Dublin.

However, I digress. The business in hand is the Barbarians against South Africa. That was the third time I had played for the Baa-Baas against international opposition. The first occasion had been against New Zealand at Twickenham in 1991, followed by the game against the Kiwis two years later. We met the Springboks in similar circumstances to the game against the New Zealanders. Specifically, we had taken a beating from New Zealand at Murrayfield and then I had captained the Barbarians against them in Cardiff. Similarly, Scotland had not performed well against South Africa and, with the Barbarians, I was presented with a timely opportunity to redress the balance. Despite the fact that these Barbarians matches against full international sides are looked upon very much as the extra Test match by tourists, there is not the same pressure with the Baa-Baas as there is when you are representing your country.

My fellow Scots in the side, in which 11 countries were represented, were Rob Wainwright and Craig Chalmers. We acquitted ourselves well, although for me the game represented a bit of a personal disaster because I pulled a hamstring which meant that I was not going to be able to fight for my place in the Scotland side which, as we now know, was under threat following the Murrayfield game against Francois Pienaar's Springboks.

Popps looked after us in regal fashion that night in Dublin and ensured that a constant supply of Guinness was on hand. One of the game's real characters, I can never think of Nick without conjuring up in my mind's eye a photograph of him immediately after the Lions' victory in the second Test in New Zealand. He is wearing a grin of Cheshire cat proportions which just shows how much that win meant to him. On that tour he also adopted the persona of Father Popplewell, a rather worldly and careworn father confessor and priest who ministered to the errant members of his flock on each Sunday throughout the tour.

The one and only Kenny Milne is my hooker and our destination is Darwin, Australia. When we were there with Scotland in 1992 the temperature was 36 degrees centigrade and, allied to the jet-lag which resulted from our long-haul flight from the UK, it was a pretty rude awakening to what lay in store for us in Oz. It wasn't the most successful tour in the history of Scottish rugby. There was a new coaching set-up in Richie Dixon and David Johnston, and David got a lot out of the backs and Richie, who in my opinion has turned into a superb Scotland coach, learnt a lot on that tour which was to stand him in good stead in the years ahead.

Kenny Milne is one of those players who is as honest as the day is long. He is one of life's good guys. In Darwin he and Rob

Wainwright had disappeared to indulge their other passion, which is angling. They had gone sea-fishing but, unknown to them, the time of a scheduled team meeting had been advanced by half an hour.

The players at the meeting watched through the hotel windows as Kenny and Rob sauntered back from the beach without a care in the world. Missing a team meeting on tour is tantamount to breaking wind in public, and we decided that they would have to be punished for their absence. Two days later they were hauled before the players' court where they were charged with cruelty to fish. They were found guilty, and the punishment was to equip themselves with polythene bags filled with water into which were placed half a dozen plastic fish which we had bought from a toy shop. Kenny and Rob, under threat of further punishment if they demurred, were then instructed to carry these polythene bags and plastic fish with them constantly for the next 48 hours.

Now that Kenny has retired we shall never again be privileged to enjoy his unique rendition of the Queen song *Bohemian Rhapsody*. It was his party piece and he has entertained the troops with it all over the world. His delivery is unique in that while he sings he also removes his clothes. Strange, I know, but he is a Herioter after all. Usually, when *Bohemian Rhapsody* time comes along, Kenny and his audience have taken a slight refreshment. However, there was one occasion on which he had to perform the piece in all of its disrobed glory when stone-cold sober. Shortly after the 1995 World Cup I had invited him along as a celeb guest to the Edinburgh Publicity Club annual lunch. The Pub Club is an organisation for people working in the advertising industry and the media, and some of their lunches are legend. Kenny was persuaded to give us his party piece, including the strip to his rather large Y-fronts, and it was with much hilarity that I picked up one of the tabloid papers the following day and saw a photograph of Kenny, microphone in hand, in a state of undress. No hiding-place, and Kenny had some explaining to do to his wife, whom he had assured that he had been to a sedate business lunch.

Completing my front row is Kenny's big – and I mean big – brother Iain. The Bear has become one of the legends of Scottish and world rugby. When I first got into the Scotland side Iain had been there for years, and he was another of my boyhood heroes. He was an immensely destructive scrummager who fought a constant battle with the scales. It was always a matter of some interest within the squad as to whether he would be over or under 20 stone and he always breathed a sigh of relief when they produced scales which did not register above the 20-stone mark. He was safe for another wee while.

The destination for The Bear is Paris. It is a beautiful city and for too long now I have promised Jenny that we will go there together. We had actually made tentative plans to spend some time together there in 1995 following the Scotland game but, as I have already mentioned, I was dropped – or as I prefer it, omitted – and the trip was off. We will do it soon, Jenny, I promise. But with Iain, the year is 1987 which was when I made my first visit to the Parc des Princes. I travelled somewhat tentatively because Colin Deans, John Rutherford and Iain had told me that as the youngest member of the team I had to adhere to tradition and get up onto the stage at the *Folies Bergère* when the side made its official visit to the night club.

The game in that special Parc des Princes atmosphere was an absolute thriller which we lost 28–22 and Iain was involved in a titanic struggle up front. I also played in the same side as him in New Zealand in 1990 but my favourite Bear story occurred in Bucharest in 1986 when, after the game, he had decided that he was going to have a night on the red wine. The Bear and red wine is a dangerous combination. He accosted the SRU president Gordon Masson and decided that the presidential white shirt, gleaming like a Persil advert, was letting the side down. This he rectified by the simple expedient of emptying a glass of vino over the president. Gordon, with great grace, said nothing but went to his room to change. He reappeared wearing another immaculate white shirt which came in for the same treatment. Iain continued drinking throughout the night and was feeling very much the worse for wear the following morning when, euphemistically put, he became ill on the bus which was taking us to the airport. He had the presence of mind to make use of a handy plastic bag and, despite the fact that we had been ordered by the Romanian authorities to remain on the bus for security reasons, Iain felt he had to get some fresh air. Carrying his plastic bag with him he became involved in conversation with a rather attractive female policewoman. He thought he was making a fine impression but, unknown to him, the plastic bag which he was by now swinging in his hand, had a number of holes in it and the contents were splattering all over the lady copper's pristine uniform.

Naughty, but nice – unless you happened to be propping against him – would be the perfect description of the Bear.

Moving on to the boilerhouse, one of my locks is going to be the Frenchman Olivier Roumat and our destination is Cardiff, where we played together for the Barbarians against New Zealand in 1993. He is a superb player and a gent even if he does, for some inexplicable reason, greet Gavin and me always with the declaration: 'Hello, Hasteengs, you bastaard.' Before the game, the Baa-Baas' secretary Geoff Windsor-Lewis, allowed me as captain to take the team out to one of Cardiff's top restaurants for a slap-up meal. Olivier was in charge of the wine and he picked the most marvellous selection to go with each course, including the pudding.

The Barbarians had issued smart new track suits for that game to which the players had rather taken a fancy. Baa-Baas president Mickey Steel-Bodger was adamant that the kit would have to be returned after the match. Olivier in particular was very keen to take the track suit home with him, his only complaint being that the trousers were a little on the short side. Mickey had said that we could keep the track suits if we won but we played so well and came so close to victory that the players put me under pressure to allow them to keep the kit. I put it to a vote and they agreed unanimously that the track suits were going home with them. Mickey was not best pleased but accepted the decision with good grace.

However, the sting in the tale happened when I got back to Edinburgh and was emptying my kit-bag to put the track suit into the washing machine. I recognised immediately that I had the wrong track suit bottoms and remembered equally quickly that Olivier, who had been complaining about his being too small, had been changing next to me. The bugger had nicked mine. Before putting the kit into the wash I checked the pockets and found £40 which Olivier had left. Nae luck Olivier. Your Barbarians track suit cost you 40 quid!

Olivier is without doubt a world-class player who, despite having had his ups and downs with the French hierarchy over the years, would be a first-choice lock in any team which I was picking. We resumed our friendship in South Africa during the 1995 World Cup when, after our heartbreaking defeat by the French in Pretoria, Olivier accompanied me to a bar called, appropriately, Le Frog, where he celebrated and I drowned my sorrows. He never got his money back.

Partnering the Frenchman in the second row is another Scottish rugby legend, Alistair McHarg. My very first visit to Murrayfield was in 1975 when I watched Scotland battle it out against Ireland and here was this huge guy in the forwards who kept on appearing alongside Andy Irvine in the backs. He was one of the players that I would always try to tap on the back when we took part in the cavalry charge from the schoolboys' enclosure at the end of every game.

I met Big Al for the first time in 1988 shortly after our game against Australia when I was invited by his London Scottish colleague Andy Cushing to play in the Dubai Sevens for a team called the Huggy Bee Thistles. The side was named after Hugh (Huggy) Bowman (Bee) who helped to sponsor the trip. Alistair was the coach and a splendid time was had by all. Watsonians had been going through a particularly lean spell and it was a great boost to my confidence to get out to Dubai and play in the sunshine. My confidence was further boosted when we got through to the final where we defeated the Welsh Crawshays.

During the final, Iain Morrison, the ex-Scotland flanker who was a member of our team, took me aside and said that Mark Titley, the Welsh fly-half whom I was marking, always broke off his left foot. Just after half-time the Crawshays won a ball near their line and Titley, sure enough, was shaping to come in off his left foot. I hit the gap that he was going to step into and almost cut him in half. If he had kept running he would have scored at the other end, but, acting on Iain's advice, I had stopped him dead in his tracks. Alistair was in command throughout that sojourn in the Gulf sunshine. Nothing was ever too much trouble for him and he makes up my second row.

Now for the back row, and I have decided to cheat here just a little. Having picked two of my brothers I can't really leave out the third, so Graeme, who, it has to be said, has bulked up somewhat from his Scottish Schoolboys days and therefore is beginning to look like a flanker, is one of my wing-forwards. Our destination is Sydney, where he came to visit when I was out there with the Lions and Scotland. Graeme, who of course now lives in Australia, has been a steadfast supporter of Gavin and me over the years and, really, it is rugby which has allowed us to get together with him on something approaching a regular basis.

After Scotland's Sydney Test against the Wallabies in 1992 we met up with Graeme and another expat, Watsonian Steven Gilhooley, who was responsible for me getting those 'speed stripes' cut into my hair during the 1989 Lions tour. Jackson's of George Street was the chosen watering-hole and, as the sabbath was approaching, we bent the 'Bundy on a Sunday' rule by a few hours for a night of relaxed reminiscences.

Sydney was a marvellous venue. We stayed in the Manly Pacific Hotel which sits by the beach like a setting from *Home and Away* – not that I ever watch it – and just around the corner was the Manly Oval where David Johnston took the backs for an extra session before the Test match. It was hard work in the Sydney sunshine, but we got our reward when we jogged back towards the hotel, jumped the wall, ran across the sand, stripped off and plunged straight into the ocean. It sure beat a cold shower and underlined yet again the fact that rugby really is a game which benefits from being played in the summer, with the sun on your back.

My open-side flanker is Finlay Calder. Fin captained both Scotland and the Lions and was an inspirational figure in both set-ups. Our touring destination is Rotorua in New Zealand, not because we have ever played a game of rugby there, but because that was where the 15 of us who stayed on in New Zealand for a short while after the 1990 tour began our holiday. White-water rafting, medicinal hot-springs to ease tired and aching limbs and 15 dollar-a-night accommodation in the Sportsman's Hotel. We didn't know at the time that Fin had got a deal with the New Zealand Rugby Union which would have got us union rates in virtually any hotel in the land. We could have stayed in the Hilton for 30 dollars-a-night! After having been at the centre of attention for the five weeks of the tour we were enjoying our anonymity. We had gone out for a Chinese meal and Fin had just remarked how wonderful it was not to be greeted by pipes and drums everywhere we went. We got back to the Sportsman's Hotel and there was the local pipe band, which had just heard that we were in town, waiting to play us back into our digs.

This was supposed to be Fin's Scottish swansong. He was retiring after we had been to New Zealand in 1990 but, despite getting the farewell gifts and sitting through all the farewell speeches, he was lured out of the shortest retirement in international history to play a full part in the World Cup the following year. He is a great character and was a great player and captain who, like all recent captains of

Scotland, led by example from the front and we would have followed him anywhere.

The final player in the team is Doddie Weir, who is going to play in his favoured position of No. 8. Bill McLaren in his TV commentaries has often likened Doddie's running style to that of a mad giraffe. Now this is appropriate because Doddie's tour destination is somewhere where he will be very much at home.

As I mentioned earlier, during the 1995 World Cup, the Scotland team were hosted by Famous Grouse for two unbelievable days at the Mala Mala game reserve nearby the Kruger National Park on the Botswanan border. I had always said that if I ever made it to South Africa then I wanted to go to a game reserve to see the wildlife in its natural habitat. We left for the trip after the disappointment of losing to France and so it was a perfect way to recharge the batteries for the quarter-final clash with New Zealand the following week.

Mala Mala has to be the most exclusive and restful destination that any of my rugby travels have taken me to. Chic doesn't begin to describe it. Despite being set deep in the bush we were cosseted in five-star luxury. Elton John and Claudia Schiffer were previous tenants of my room so I can truthfully claim to have shared a bed with Claudia but not Elton. He had Ian Jadine's bed.

Doddie has come a long way since he made his debut in 1990. We called him Bambi in those days and despite his still-tender years he is currently Scotland's most capped forward and it wouldn't surprise me in the slightest if Doddie were to go on to take the outright Scottish record. He is a character of the type that everyone says no longer exists in the game. He has it in him to become a forward of genuine world class. He has time on his side and I sincerely hope that we haven't yet seen the best of him.

So that's my team. We're guaranteed good crack, great company and we might even play a bit of rugby as well, and once we've completed our round of world destinations I'm going to take them to Sun City in South Africa. There we will team up with the Sun City Scots who hosted us so magnificently during the World Cup in 1995. We would stay in the Lost City Hotel and play a few rounds of golf. My team would also be the judges to the Miss World contest before heading to Mala Mala for a bit of extra R and R. What a tour. Would anyone like to sponsor it?

Statistics

1986	France	Murrayfield	18–17
	Wales	Cardiff	15–22
	England	Murrayfield	33–6
	Ireland	Dublin	10–9
	Romania	Bucharest	33–18
1987	Ireland	Murrayfield	16–12
	France	Paris	22–28
	Wales	Murrayfield	21–15
	Romania (RWC)	Dunedin	55–28
1988	Ireland	Dublin	18–22
	France	Murrayfield	23–12
	Wales	Cardiff	20–25
	Australia	Murrayfield	13–32
1989	Wales	Murrayfield	23–7
	England	Twickenham	12–12
	Ireland	Murrayfield	37–21
	France	Paris	3–19
	Fiji	Murrayfield	38–17
	Romania	Murrayfield	32–0
1990	Ireland	Dublin	13–10
	France	Murrayfield	21–0
	Wales	Cardiff	13–9

	England	Murrayfield	13–7
	New Zealand	Dunedin	16–31
	New Zealand	Auckland	18–31
	Argentina	Murrayfield	49–3
1991	France	Paris	9–15
	Wales	Murrayfield	32–12
	England	Twickenham	12–21
	Ireland	Murrayfield	28–25
	Japan (RWC)	Murrayfield	47–9
	Zimbabwe (RWC)	Murrayfield	51–12
	Ireland(RWC)	Murrayfield	24–15
	Western Samoa (RWC)	Murrayfield	28–6
	England (RWC)	Murrayfield	6–9
	New Zealand (RWC)	Cardiff	6–13
1992	England	Murrayfield	7–25
	Ireland	Dublin	18–10
	France	Murrayfield	10–6
	Wales	Cardiff	12–15
	Australia	Sydney	12–27
	Australia	Brisbane	13–27
1993	Ireland	Murrayfield	15–3
	France	Paris	3–11
	Wales	Murrayfield	20–0
	England	Twickenham	12–26
	New Zealand	Murrayfield	15–51
1994	England	Murrayfield	14–15
	Ireland	Dublin	6–6
	France	Murrayfield	12–20

1995	South Africa	Murrayfield	10–34
	Wales	Murrayfield	26–13
	England	Twickenham	12–24
	Romania (R)	Murrayfield	49–16
	Tonga(RWC)	Pretoria	41–5
	France (RWC)	Pretoria	19–23
	New Zealand (RWC)	Pretoria	30–48
1996	Ireland	Dublin	16–10
	France	Murrayfield	19–14
	Wales	Cardiff	16–14
	England	Murrayfield	9–18
	New Zealand	Auckland	12–36

OTHER MAJOR REPRESENTATIVE MATCHES

1989	Barbarians v New Zealand	Twickenham	10–21
	Lions v France	Paris	29–27
1991	Scotland v Barbarians	Murrayfield	16–16
1993	Barbarians v New Zealand (Cpt.)	Cardiff	12–25
1994	Barbarians v South Africa	Dublin	23–15

MAJOR TOURS

1987	World Cup
1989	British Lions to Australia
1990	Scotland to New Zealand
1991	World Cup
1992	Scotland to Australia
1993	British Lions to New Zealand
1995	World Cup
1996	Scotland to New Zealand

THE TEAMS

George Watson's College, Scottish Schools, Watsonians, Newcastle Northern, Anglo-Scots, Northumberland, Edinburgh, Barbarians, Scotland, British Lions.

BARBARIANS APPEARANCES (Non-internationals)

1986 v Newport
1989 v East Midlands
1990 v Cardiff
1993 v Exeter
1989 Represented Barbarians at Hong Kong Sevens.

CAREER LANDMARKS

● Set new Scottish record of 62 appearances in major internationals in second Test against New Zealand at Eden Park, Auckland, 22:6:96. Scott and brother Gavin had held the record jointly until then.

● He and Gavin are the only brothers ever to have played together in a British Lions' Test match. Australia 1989.

● Scott and Sean Lineen hold the world record for a Test centre partnership with 28 appearances together.

● Scott and Gavin made their Scotland debuts together against France in 1986 and won their 50th caps together, again against France, in 1994.

● Captained Watsonians to rare, back-to-back victories at Gala and Melrose Sevens, 1996.